Photo by Standish and Preece, N.Z.

M.A. Rugby Pratt

THE PIONEERING DAYS
OF
SOUTHERN MAORILAND

BY

M. A. RUGBY PRATT

PRESIDENT-ELECT N.Z. METHODIST CONFERENCE, 1932,
CONNEXIONAL SECRETARY AND AUTHORIZED REPRESENTA-
TIVE METHODIST CHURCH OF NEW ZEALAND,
CUSTODIAN OF DEEDS AND EARLY RECORDS,
&C. &C. &C.

'VETERIS NON INSCIUS AEVI'
(Not unmindful of the past)

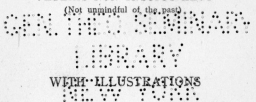

WITH ILLUSTRATIONS

LONDON
THE EPWORTH PRESS
J. ALFRED SHARP

First Edition, 1932

MADE AND PRINTED BY
THE DEVONSHIRE PRESS, 64 FLEET STREET, TORQUAY,
ENGLAND

TO THE MEMORY OF
MY MOTHER

Who early taught me to love
Good Men and Good Things;

AND TO

MY WIFE

The Truest and Trustiest
of Yokemates,
For help unfailing,

I DEDICATE THIS BOOK

CONTENTS

CHAP.   PAGE

I.   BY WAY OF INTRODUCTION . . . 13

II.   THE TATTOOED TRIBES OF TUMUKI . . 19

III.   SOUTHERN SEA KINGS AND A SULLIED SCROLL   27

IV.   THE TUSSLE WITH TE RAUPARAHA . . 36

V.   THE COMING OF THE PIONEER PREACHER . 47

VI.   THE HERALD OF A HIGHER RACE . . 56

VII.   BRITISH BEGINNINGS AND PAKEHA PASSIONS   64

VIII.   GAMESOME GODS AND CARICATURES OF DEITY   76

IX.   HAUNTING SHAPES OF HORROR . . . 86

X.   A WHALING STATION IN THE FIERY FORTIES . 96

XI.   THE LABYRINTH OF THE LANGUAGE . . 108

XII.   WINNING AN UPWARD WAY . . . 118

XIII.   TRAVELS OF THE TRAIL-BLAZER . . . 128

XIV.   THE PATH OF POMPALLIER AND THE TRAIL OF
        TAMIHANA 139

XV.   THE NARROW ARITHMETIC OF SECTARIANISM 148

XVI.   BISHOP SELWYN'S SOUTHWARD EXCURSION . 157

XVII.   RECORDS OF THE RANGATIRAS . . . 165

XVIII.   TRANSFORMING MAORI CHARACTER . . 174

XIX.   NOBLE SERVICE ON A NARROW STAGE . 183

XX.   PREPARING FOR A NEW COLONIZATION . 195

XXI.   CHARLES CREED AND THE SCOTTISH SETTLE-
        MENT 202

XXII.   BY WAY OF CONCLUSION 213

       GLOSSARY OF MAORI WORDS . . . 217

       INDEX 219

LIST OF ILLUSTRATIONS

1. THE AUTHOR . . . . FRONTISPIECE

FACING PAGE

2. THE COMING OF THE MAORI 16
3. THE ARRIVAL OF THE MAORI FROM HAWAIKI . 24
4. THINKING OF OTHER DAYS 32
5. A TYPICAL OLD MAORI 41
6. THE HOBART TOWN WHALING SHIP *DERWENT HUNTER* 48
7. THE HOBART TOWN WHALING SHIP *PACIFIC* . 57
8. TE RAUPARAHA—AN OLD MAORI WARRIOR . 64
9. A MAORI WAR CANOE 72
10. REV. JAMES WATKIN 80
11. CAPTAIN HOBSON, R.N. 89
12. TAMATI WAAKA NENE 89
13. WHALERS AND FRENCH WARSHIPS AT PORT OTAGO IN 1840 97
14. THE ANCHORAGE AT OTAGO HEADS IN 1840 . 105
15. WESLEYAN MISSION HOUSE AT WAIKOUAITI, 1840 113
16. SIGNATURES OF MAORI CHIEFS AND TEACHERS, 1841 120
17. THE FIRST ENTRIES IN THE FIRST MARRIAGE REGISTER, 1841 129
18. A MOERAKI MAORI 136

                                                    FACING PAGE

19.   THE FAMOUS MOERAKI BOULDERS   .   .   .   136

20.   A TYPICAL PIONEER HOME   145

21.   A MAORI SWING   152

22.   THE MOKO SIGNATURE OF TUHAWAIKI, 1840   .   168

23.   MR. JOHN JONES   176

24.   TE MATENGA TAIAROA   176

25.   REV. J. F. H. WOHLERS   192

26.   REV. CHARLES CREED   208

FOREWORD

THIS book will appeal to its readers as a vivid and faithful account of arduous, pioneering days, when the foundations of Empire were being laid in New Zealand and a tone was imparted to the country's life which the passing years have not obliterated. The men and women of those times were of the best colonizing stock. They had courage and initiative and displayed untiring industry and unwavering tenacity of purpose. Braving, in meagre craft, the perils of their far voyage, they came to a life poor and mean in all material things, but this they faced with hearts rich in mingled fortitude and hope. And we to-day enter into their labours and share the fruit of their sacrifice, who dwell with every aspect of comfort and convenience in the broadening cities which they founded and upon the lands which they began to till.

The Christian Church was here at the early dawn of the day. The Anglican and Methodist Missions long preceded the Treaty of Waitangi by which, with the free consent of the Maori people, the land came under the governance of the Queen, and the influence of the missionaries was a considerable factor in favour of British rule. The earliest settlers, as they arrived, even when accompanied by ministers of religion, thus found waiting them the grasp of friendly hands and the ministry of godly men.

It is the purpose of this volume to re-tell the story of those days in 'Southern Maoriland,' that we, who have entered into so great a heritage, may cultivate an honourable pride in the fathers whose memory is here so fittingly revived, and that those of other lands, who share our race

and speech, may learn by what visions and labours a new
Britain has arisen beneath the Southern Cross.

The author has every qualification for the work he has
undertaken. He is well-known among us as possessing
the gifts and enthusiasms of the historian. The present
writer well remembers a peerless morning some few years
ago spent under his guidance on the curving sands of
Waikouaiti Bay, and in examining the remains of the
old Mission Station and of the whaling settlement at
Karitane Peninsula, Mount Watkin all the time command-
ing the far background. It was a memorable day during
which the author revealed his mastery of every detail
of that long-past life. The fuller and wider record which
this volume contains is marked by a like competence and,
as the story unfolds, it lacks none of that colour and
realistic movement which such a hand alone can impart.

C. H. LAWS, B.A., D.D.,
Ex-Principal and Foundation Fellow
of Trinity College.

Auckland, N.Z.
July 7, 1931.

Chapter I

BY WAY OF INTRODUCTION

Can you hear the great wheels turning ?
Can you see God's lightning burning
    In the tireless dynamo ?
Can you catch the hum of power ?
Catch the Keynote of the hour ?

God's own hands these wheels are turning
God's own heart this fire burning !
    The eternal Dynamo !

There is in most men an instinct of historic curiosity that prompts them to peer into the past. Many of the figures of that past and much of the fact and incident that made up its life lie buried deep in unawaking sleep. But though some of the doers and many of their deeds are gulfed in oblivion no fate of forgetfulness can befall the principles they exalted and the benefits they won.

Quite a considerable body of literature has laid bare the treasure-trove of history and of romance with which the story of New Zealand abounds, but no volume has yet appeared that deals adequately with that period in the history of the Province of Otago immediately prior to the founding of the Presbyterian Free Church Settlement in 1848. Dr. Robert McNab in *The Old Whaling Days* and Dr. T. M. Hocken in his *Contributions to the Early History of New Zealand*, have given only a bare outline of the throbbing activities of the former half of the nineteenth century. The data for a fuller chronicle did not lie to their hand. Much of it was comprised in manuscript journals, diaries, letters and missionary reports that were in private hands in England and Australia as well as in New Zealand. The search for that material has been, for the present writer, a labour of love.

In the absence of an authentic history of the fast receding years prior to the founding of the Scottish Settlement many legends have gained currency. Some of the legends are suspended only on slender threads that hang from the broken meshes of memory. Others have travelled down the years by the precarious vehicle of oral tradition, tradition recited, perchance, by those not themselves eye-witnesses of the happenings they relate, and at times having little save its antiquity to commend it to credence.

If history is to receive its true interpretation one must first get at the facts of the story and see vividly the picture of the past. The origins of the history of Otago are not lost in the dawnless night of time and there need be no mist of ignorance lying within the folds of its far-stretching horizons. The story to be told in the chapters that follow rests on the solid strata of historical reality. Nothing set down in the record has been taken for granted and nothing furnished by fancy. The author has sought to see reality and has striven to avoid alike the errors of antiquarianism and the allurements of mere impressionism. The facts set forth have been drawn mainly from contemporary records of actual participants in and observers of the events recorded. Reciting as they do the personal reactions of the pioneers to the doings of their day, these chronicles should possess a measure of that vividness and vitality which do not ordinarily accompany mere compilations of data by purely objective historians. Of course there are gaps in the story and the blanks are sufficiently roomy to provide a spacious play-house for the imagination of the individual reader, who may, at his own caprice, indulge in an exercise the writer has not permitted himself.

The author's first interest in the Maori race was stimulated in early boyhood by the tales his father and mother had to tell of Te Kooti and his wild Hauhaus

whose raids on the settlements at Poverty Bay and elsewhere struck terror to the hearts of the white settlers.
Then in the days of very early youth it was the privilege
of the writer, who had gone with his parents to Hobart,
Tasmania, often to spend long hours listening to the
thrilling recital of tales of long ago from the lips of the
aged missionary, Samuel Ironside, who, in the forties of
last century played so conspicuously noble a part in
connexion with the events preceding the Wairau Massacre
which inaugurated the long and tragic conflict between
the brown and the white races in New Zealand.

The writer also enjoyed the friendship of the Rev.
George Clarke, sometime Chancellor of the University of
Tasmania, who had, in early life, played an important part
in some of the most stirring events in New Zealand history.
Mr. Clarke's father, formerly a missionary at Kerikeri,
had been placed at the head of the Native Department
when the seat of Government was established at Auckland.
The son won distinction as an interpreter on a critical
occasion at the very first criminal sitting of a Supreme
Court in New Zealand. He was then only a lad of twenty,
but so pleased was Governor Hobson with his understanding
of the Maori mind that he appointed the youth Protector
of the native race. In that capacity he withstood the
subtle and imperious Colonel Wakefield. After the Wairau
Massacre in 1843 he acted as interpreter for Governor
FitzRoy and conveyed to the Maoris the Governor's
decision that the English were in the wrong because they
provoked the conflict by forcibly taking possession of
disputed lands while the case was actually under debate,
and that they were further to blame in that they sent
an armed party to arrest the Chiefs on a trivial pretext,
and at the last moment were the first to fire. In 1844
Mr. Clarke participated in the negotiations for the sale
by the Maoris of the land for the Otago Scottish Settlement,
and the Deed of Purchase is in his handwriting.

The interest aroused by such contacts was stimulated

during student days at Queen's College, University of
Melbourne, when it was the writer's frequent privilege,
in the home of Mr. Florence Gardiner at St. Kilda, a
great-uncle who had lived in Auckland during and after
the days of Governor Hobson, to glean other facts of New
Zealand history. In this home he often met the Rev.
Edwin Iredale Watkin, D.D., a son of the pioneer missionary
to the Maoris of the South Island of New Zealand, who
delighted to find an interested listener to his tales of dimly
distant days in Maoriland.

In course of time it fell to the lot of the writer to exercise
his ministry near to the scenes where the Rev. James
Watkin planted the first Christian banner in the South
Island of New Zealand, an area over which, for a while,
he had ecclesiastical jurisdiction as Chairman of the
Otago-Southland District of the Methodist Church of New
Zealand. Still later the writer had the opportunity to
spend some weeks in company with another son of the
pioneer missionary—the Rev. Jabez Bunting Watkin—
both in his home in Tonga and also in the small cutter,
the *Fetuu Aho*, in which for sixteen days they together
sailed the stormy and reef-strewn waters that lave the
Friendly Islands, days in which Mr. Watkin beguiled the
hours with stories of his father's life and work in New
Zealand, with which country some of his own richest
memories were associated.

From the sources mentioned a mass of material has
accumulated throughout the years. It has been no easy
task to disentangle from this mass the threads of history
and to weave them into a clear unbiassed narrative, which,
whilst omitting no essential facts, should be instinct with
life and calculated to carry the reader along with unflagging
interest. It was at Waikouaiti, in the Province of Otago,
where daylight broke on the dark Maori race of the South
Island of New Zealand. Here, in 1840, the Wesleyan
Methodist Missionary stood at the fountain-head of the
history of that southern region. His work and that of

'THE COMING OF THE MAORI.'

his successor—Charles Creed—transformed a land, devil-dark and blood-soaked, into one in which now flourish stately things, that, but for them, might never have been. The rich civilization of to-day stands elevated on the graves of these pioneer preachers. It was they who were the real trail-blazers. Later men might be greater men, but the first must ever remain the first. They did what no other had done before and what no others could do again. To give them more enduring date these chapters in that rough island's story may, in some measure, serve.

The indebtedness of the writer to others is greater than can be recorded, but special thanks are due to various members of the Watkin family for letters and papers relating to the period; to the librarians of the Hocken and the McNab libraries in Dunedin; the Alexander Turnbull Library in Wellington and the Mitchell Library in Sydney, for making available the resources of those institutions. The works of Mr. Elsdon Best, Mr. James Cowan, Mr. Lindsay Buick and others have sometimes been used to check the writer's own results.

It remains but to add that the task of garbing these 'waifs of history' in 'the goodly ornature of well-apparelled speech' has only been faultily performed. The leisureless life of a church administrator weighted with great and multiplying official responsibilities has offered little opportunity to fashion the available material into choicest literary form, and often the imp of discouragement has whispered counsel to abandon the project.

That this record is now ready for a literary seed-sowing is due not only to personal desire and to a sense of public duty, but also, in some measure, to the persistent plea of two personal friends now no longer living, the Hon. Robert McNab, M.A., LL.D., whose sun set in life's early afternoon, and Sir George Fenwick, K.B., whose long life's day closed amid the richness of autumnal splendours. Both these gentlemen in different ways did much to preserve authentic records of days beyond recall and also to encourage others

B

to glean historical harvests before the onrushing years
had gulfed them in the silent deeps of oblivion.

To my brother, Mr. A. W. Courtney Pratt, of Hobart,
Tasmania, I am also indebted for the pictures of the whaling
ships, *Derwent Hunter* and *Pacific*, as well as for much
encouragement.

Chapter II

THE TATTOOED TRIBES OF TUMUKI

Here once the mighty Atua had his dwelling, in mystery,
And hence weird sounds were heard at midnight, swelling,
    across the sea.
Here once the Haka sounded ; and din of battle shook the grey
    crags :
Triumphant shout, and agonised death rattle startled the
    shags.
Gone is the Atua, and the hillsides lonely, the warriors dead ;
No sight, no sound ! The weird, wild wailing only of gull
    instead.
All undisturbed the Pakeha's herds are creeping along the hill ;
On lazy tides the Pakeha's ships are sleeping, and all is still.
                                        —Dora Wilcox.

New Zealand is a land rich in romance. The stirring
story of Ao-tea-roa, to give that country its ancient name,
is preserved in history and tradition, in legend and in
myths that reach back to dimly distant centuries. The
mythical epoch of Maoriland is represented by sundry
attempts to preserve the recollection of events and personalities, the guarantee of whose reality is only of the very
vaguest. These myths tell the tale of this territory when
it was in possession of the race of giant Kahui Tipua
ogres, reputed to be endowed with supernatural powers
such as the capacity to stride from mountain to mountain,
to swallow rivers and to transform themselves into any
shape or substance that caprice might suggest.

Following this fabulous age comes the period of legendary
lore, itself sufficiently remote to render impossible the task
of telling where fact is overlaid with futile fancy. Associated with this period are shadowy tales of aboriginal

dwellers along the east coast of the South Island, people
of peaceful and non-carnivorous habits, so far as human
flesh is concerned, who roamed the island and hunted the
moa, ere yet the Hawaikians guided their canoes to the
coasts of the land of the long white cloud.

Next comes the period of tradition dating approximately
from the middle of the fifteenth century. This period
gives the story, all too scanty in its outlines, that has been
orally transmitted from generation to generation, of the
Hawaiki emigrants who came from a land whose exact
location is as yet undetermined, steering their canoes across
the trackless sea, without chart or compass, sextant,
chronometer or nautical almanac. These old-time navi-
gators, guided by sun and stars, at last landed on the shores
of Ao-tea-roa and shared the life of the aboriginal dwellers
until their multiplying numbers gave them ascendancy.
On one of the canoes, the Arawa, which is said to have
found a haven on the east coast of the North Island, was
a Hawaikian named Waitaha. He founded a tribe which,
after varying vicissitudes in the North, crossed the straits
of Raukawa (Cook Strait) that separate the two islands,
and in the South, amidst conditions of peace and plenty,
lived in enjoyment until the tribe was, save for a small
remnant, exterminated by the merciless Ngatimamoe tribe,
which is said to have invaded the country towards the
middle of the sixteenth century. This tribe multiplied
and divided into hapus which held scattered positions,
including some along the Otago coastline. During the
blood-red years of the Ngatimamoe occupancy the island
was made a veritable place of skulls. Dark intrigue, plot
and counterplot, savage warfare and greedy cannibalism
abounded, until Nemesis, in the shape of the Ngai-Tahu
tribe, displaced a fierce and treacherous race, whose
record of rapine and slaughter was relieved only by rarest
displays of magnanimity or of mercy.

The period of shadowy tradition carries us through the
sanguinary Ngai-Tahu domination until towards the close

of the seventeenth century, when the outlines of out-standing personalities and of events become clearer. About the time of the visit of Abel Janszoon Tasman in 1642, the traditional era merges into the period of actual history in which statements of provable facts, with defin-itely attested dates, are regularly set forth. The Ngai-Tahu, like their predecessors, came from the North to the South Island, which they called Tumuki, and settling first at Wairau, gradually exterminated or absorbed the Ngati-mamoe tribe, and, pressing down the east coast, occupied fortified positions in many strategic centres.

Few parts of the ancient Tumuki, or Te-Wai-Pounamu, as the South Island was subsequently called by the Maoris, have a more romantic record than gathers around the sea-swept shores that stretch from Moeraki to the region of Foveaux Strait. Tradition says that it was near the long beach that stretches south-west of Moeraki to Mata-kaea (Shag Point) that the canoe ' Te-Arai-te-uru,' in which the ancestors of the Ngai-Tahu tribe came from Hawaiki, was caught in a storm and wrecked. The ' Moeraki boulders ' that here strew the foreshore, are said to be the petrified eel baskets and calabashes from the ill-fated canoe. The canoe itself, turned to stone, lies also at the mouth of the Waihemo River, with its petrified commander still on board !

Of the whole southern coastline, however, perhaps no portion is so rich in its associations as the graceful, curving outline of Waikouaiti Bay (known to the ancient Maori as Ohinetemoa), and the bold promonotory known as Matainaka Head at its northern extremity, together with the picturesque Karitane Peninsula which forms the southern arm of the bay. For ages the liquid acres of the South Pacific Ocean, tossing to the sportive winds, have rolled upon the silver sands of Waikouaiti Bay, and sung their mighty anthem to the scarped and battlemented cliffs of Karitane and Matainaka. For ages too, native tribes have dwelt on the narrow strip of territory that stretches from the foreshore to the heights of old Hikororoa, that noble cenotaph which has seen many a generation hand on the torch of life to its successor, and which still rears itself so proudly in the background.

It is interesting to record that Hikororoa, by decree of the local tribes about the year 1844, was re-named ' Mount Watkin ' to keep green the memory of James Watkin, the Wesleyan missionary who inaugurated the first Christian mission in the South Island of New Zealand. Karitane Peninsula was not always so called. For centuries it bore the name of Huriawa, which means ' the diverted river.' In bygone ages the Waikouaiti stream, which probably derives its euphonious name from the ' greater and the lesser waters ' that converge as they flow to the ocean at the base of the peninsula, did not run into the sea, as it now does, on the north-west, but on the south-west side of old Huriawa. It was on Hautekapakapa Hill, an ancient assembly ground of the Maoris and overlooking Waikouaiti Bay that Mr. Watkin had his first mission station, in the charge of which he was succeeded in 1844 by the Rev. Charles Creed.

The name ' Karitane ' has become known to all the world through the great work done by Sir Truby King in the interests of child life by means of the Karitane nursing system. For years Dr. King had his home on the Peninsula. The question has sometimes been raised as to the source and meaning of the word ' Karitane.' In his book on Maori place names Mr. W. H. S. Roberts refers to the uncertainty of its derivation. He says that the word may be translated ' a man to dig,' or ' a bruised man,' or ' a maimed husband,' whilst some have rendered it ' where men dig.' Others have interpreted it as meaning ' swamp ground.' All of these meanings are emphatically rejected by that outstanding authority, Mr. Elsdon Best, in a letter to the present writer.

A tradition has gained wide acceptance that the old name of the peninsula was changed to Karitane to perpetuate

the name of the Rev. Charles Creed, who was known to
the Maoris as ' Kariti,' the final syllable, ' tane,' signifying
' the man.' Light is thrown upon this interesting, but
scarcely tenable suggestion, by a conversation that the
present writer had, in the year 1919, with an old Waikouaiti
resident in the person of Mrs. Mary Ann Thompson, who
was the half-caste daughter of Thomas Tandy, a Swede,
and his Maori wife, Meria Manaha. The estimable lady
had, as a child, been baptized by the Rev. James Watkin
at Waikouaiti on March 24, 1844. She stated that she
perfectly remembered the re-naming of the peninsula.
She declared that she was present at a native korero on
Hautekapakapa Hill when the noted chief, Rawiri Te
Maire, who was a Wesleyan native teacher and had been
baptized by Watkin on January 22, 1843, made the
proposal to perpetuate the name of Creed as they had
already perpetuated the name of Watkin. In support
of his proposal the chief spoke of the good work done by
both Mr. and Mrs. Creed in the interests of the Maoris,
and especially by Mrs. Creed in teaching the girls to sew
and in teaching the mothers some simple lessons in hygiene.
Mrs. Thompson said that the suggestion was acclaimed
and unanimously adopted by the assembled tribe.

One would like to think that the story of the half-caste
lady bore the indubitable seal of historicity in linking
the work of Creed the missionary with that of Dr. Truby
King. The story may have some real basis, but the philological difficulties are such as to compel the conclusion
that it lacks the essential elements to carry complete
conviction. Mr. Elsdon Best agrees that the name
' Creed ' was represented in Maori as ' Kariti,' with the
stress on the second syllable. In Maori the word for
' man ' (homo) is ' tangata.' The word ' tane ' really means
' the male ' (vir). As the Maori did not use ' portmanteau '
words in Alice in Wonderland fashion, the combination
of the words ' Kariti-tane ' as signifying ' the man Creed '
would be impossible to the true Maori. In this conclusion

Mr. Best and Mr. Johannes Andersen, another reliable authority, agree. It is a pity that a pretty story is not better supported. It is here set forth in detail because of its recurring interest. But to return to our main theme.

Karitane Peninsula, which is connected with the mainland by a low, sandy isthmus, is about a mile in length, and is formed of a succession of somewhat steep hills that terminate at the rocky and precipitous sea-swept point, known to the Maoris of a past generation as Pa Katata. Here were settled three hapus of the Ngai-Tahu tribe, namely the Ngatihuirapa, the Ngaiteruakihikihi and the Ngaiterakifakabito. It was from this centre that there radiated many of the chief influences that touched the life of Otago in the two momentous decades prior to the founding of the Scottish Free Church Settlement in the year 1848. These influences will be fully treated in subsequent chapters. Meanwhile we may turn our gaze backward for a glance at two of the principal chiefs who, some two centuries ago, won for these hapus and the Ngai-Tahu tribe generally, a position of security in their southern quarters.

In their conflict with the Ngatimamoe tribe the Ngai-Tahu natives, somewhere about the first quarter of the eighteenth century, had won a decisive battle at Moeraki, about twenty miles north, by boat, from Waikouaiti. The chiefs who led them to success were Taoka of Otakou and Te Wera, who had built a strongly fortified pa at Huriawa, the Karitane of to-day. Not satisfied with this success, Te Wera, who had a grievance against an old priest at Moeraki on account of some heretical beliefs that he had been promulgating, killed the apostate tohunga, whose cooked body made a meal for this militant champion of Maori orthodoxy and for his willing warriors. Well content with his achievements Te Wera returned to Waikouaiti. It is worthy of note that the remains of Te Wera's pa and of the Owhare kaika, with its famous carved house, Kuramatakitaki, which stood on the banks

THE ARRIVAL OF THE MAORI FROM HAWAIKI.

of the Waikouaiti river a little above the pa, were visible until a few years ago.

It was not long, however, after his return, that Te Wera was once more in the thick of conflict, this time with his uncle, the chief who had shared with him in the defeat of the Ngatimamoe and had now conceived a bitter hatred for his influential nephew. The story of the trouble has been preserved by Mr. James Cowan and may here be given in outline. Te Wera and his son Patuka, with another chief, were on a visit to the natives of Purakanui, a village on the shores of what is now called Blueskin Bay. During this visit a roving war party from Pukekura Pa at Otakou Heads surprised the villagers by night in prosecution of an ancient tribal vendetta. Te Wera and his companions, who were quartered in a raupo hut, were singled out for death. Sitting around the fire, enjoying a repast of preserved birds, they were unaware of the presence of adversaries until the sensitive ear of Te Wera detected the first whiz of a spear hurled by one of the marauders. Ducking his head just in time to avoid it, the shaft struck one of his companions, who was mortally wounded. The others, effecting their escape, meditated vengeance. Te Wera organized a canoe expedition to Otakou Heads to hunt for scalps. Surprising some women gathering flax for mat-making, he killed and beheaded them. Pointing his canoe homeward he took the satisfaction of holding up several heads as he passed the village, with a view to infuriating the unsuspecting relatives of his victims. His savage joy was complete when he heard the piercing tangi cry of the outraged hapu rending the air as they wailed for their dead. The Pukekura people resolved upon retaliation, and to gratify his own implacable hatred of his young kinsman, Taoka and his people joined forces with the Pukekura warriors. Canoe loads of braves were rallied from as far north as Timaru. Led by Taoka the combined forces laid siege to the parapeted and pallisaded hill-fort of Huriawa, which occupied a fine strategic position and commanded an extensive view of land and coastline and sea.

In anticipation of attack Te Wera had laid in supplies sufficient to withstand a siege for a year. The defences were of unusual strength and the garrison evidently a powerful one. The situation lent itself to defensive warfare. The steep cliffs and high scarped walls, surmounted by a succession of rows of stout pallisading were a good line of defence for the Huriawa people. Taoka's army pitched camp on the long island sand-spit in Waikouaiti Bay just to the north of the Pa. Here they carried out their war dances in furious fashion and hurled their angry threats at the garrison, which flung back in their teeth defiant challenges and bitter taunts. From this spot, too, they made their frequent yet fruitless assaults upon the stockade. The blockade, which lasted many long and weary months, ended in failure and Taoka's army raised the siege, leaving Te Wera with a mana considerably enhanced, much to the old uncle's chagrin.

Several years later Te Wera with many of his people left Huriawa in their sea-going canoes to settle further south. Some of the party occupied the northern shores of Teara-a-kiwa, as Foveaux Strait was then called, but Te Wera took up quarters at Ohekia, an inlet on the north-east side of Rakiura (Stewart Island). This place became known as Wehingao-te-Wera, and is now familiar as Paterson's Inlet. In later years he settled on the shores of Orako, a place known to us as Colac Bay. Here he died, lamenting that his body would go to the grave to putrify for the satisfaction of worms, rather than to the oven to provide an appetising meal for foemen worthy of so valorous a victim. His deeds, however, became incorporated in the tribal traditions and were recited amongst the various hapus of the south with whose later fortunes we shall shortly be engaged.

CHAPTER III

SOUTHERN SEA-KINGS AND A SULLIED SCROLL

I saw no use in the past : only a scene
Of degradation, imbecility
The record of disgraces best forgotten,
A sullen page in human chronicles
Fit to erase . . . .
. . . . Not so, dear child
Of after days. Wilt thou reject the past
Big with deep warnings of the proper tenure
By which thou hast the earth ?
                                      BROWNING : *Paracelsus.*

DURING the closing years of the eighteenth century ' the
smokeless seas of the new-born south ' were ploughed by
the keels of vessels in quest of the monsters of the deep.
Those that sought the cachalot in the open seas to the
north of New Zealand ordinarily made the Bay of Islands
the base of their operations, and found welcome change
from deep-sea whaling by engaging in the pursuit of the
kekeno, or seals, that basked upon our shores when they
deserted the sea for breeding purposes and for repose.

For the most part the men engaged in the industry were
of truly heroic mould, and though no Homer sings these
sea-kings of the south, and no scaldic sagas immortalize
their dauntless defiance both of the moods and the
monsters of the then uncharted deep, theirs was the spirit
that breathed in the heroes of Greece and in the Vikings
of the North, the spirit, too, that beat in the breasts of
the men who did the bidding of Blake and Drake and

Nelson. But the spirit was vagrant, and, when ashore on strange coasts, and ' their camp-fires bright had seared the night,' their wild life would range in tumult as they beguiled the hours with revel and with rout.

With such relentless thoroughness was the industry of the ' fishing ' fleet carried on, that by the year 1830 the schools of patena, or sperm whales, had become so depleted that their pursuit on the high seas had become somewhat profitless. The sealing industry, too, had dwindled to small proportions, owing either to the thinning out process, or to their departure to regions where there was less fear of molestation.

Coincident with this decline was an increased demand in the markets of the world for whalebone and for the oil of the black whales, or takena, as they were called by the South Island Maoris. This family of the cetacean tribe, it had been noted, made it their practice to visit various bays on the New Zealand coast-line in the autumn and winter for the purpose of bringing forth their young. Quick to recognize the possibility of promoting a profitable industry in this branch of their calling, the shipping merchants of Sydney and Hobart Town, who, until now, had been engaged in deep sea whaling, turned their attention to this new branch of their calling and established shore stations where the right whale was wont to rendezvous.

On the coasts of Otago the whales usually made their appearance about the end of March and probably in that month of the year 1829 the first whaling station in the South was equipped by Bunn and Company, a Sydney firm, on the shores of Preservation Inlet. To catch the season of 1832 Messrs. Weller Bros., of Sydney, fitted up a shore station in Otago Harbour, and, in addition to the necessary equipment for the whaling industry, brought from Australia six cases of muskets, sixty-two barrels of gunpowder, and stores of gin, rum and tobacco. Rum and tobacco were then recognized forms of currency and changed hands as freely as coins of the realm. The so-called rum was, says Mr. W. Pember Reeves, often but an inferior arrack—that deadliest of spirits—and with it the Sydney of those days poisoned the Pacific. Great quantities reached the whaling stations, and with demoralising results, as one would naturally expect. The hard-working whalers dissipated their earnings in grog bought from their masters, and the Maoris, who, until the advent of the white man with his waipiro (smelly-water), had no knowledge of any intoxicating beverage, were not slow to drink, to their own deeper demoralization, the liquor sold to them at the boiling-down stations. Disaster early overtook Weller Brothers' station, which was destroyed by fire in April, 1832. It was speedily refitted, however, and for several years did a thriving trade in oil, whale-bone, seal-skins, flax, potatoes and salted fish.

Until the year 1834 the Sydney and Hobart Town merchants had a virtual monopoly of the whaling trade in Otago, but in that year British and American vessels embarked upon the industry and were soon followed by the Portuguese, the Dutch and the French. The Americans and the French each had a fleet of almost a score of vessels trading in these waters, though neither they, the Dutch, nor the Portuguese set up shore stations.

It should, perhaps, be explained, that from these stations a sharp look-out was kept for the appearance of the whales, and when they were sighted, shore parties would put off in well-equipped boats that were ordinarily manned by four rowers, a steersman and a headsman. The whale was pursued, and, when overtaken, the headsman drove home the harpoon and then attacked the victim with a lance, in its vital parts. The huge body of the dead captive was then towed ashore, and hoisted on the sheerlegs to be flinched, prior to the blubber being boiled in the try-pots on the beach. Such an enterprise attracted the natives and gave scope for Maori daring. Many of the Maoris became expert headsmen and prided themselves that they were no whit behind the pakeha in the art of throwing the harpoon.

About the year 1835 Mr. John Jones, who had been a waterman in Sydney and had embarked upon several profitable undertakings, acquired a whaling station at Preservation Bay and purchased and equipped a small schooner for carrying on bay whaling. This was the Mr. ' Johnny' Jones who later became so closely identified with the early days of Otago provincial development. By the year 1839 Mr. Jones had so greatly prospered that he possessed a very considerable fleet and had acquired seven bay whaling stations between Moeraki and Preservation Bay. These gave employment to some 280 men for a good part of each year. Mr. Jones's principal station, situated at Waikouaiti, was acquired in the year just mentioned. It had been founded in 1837 by Messrs. Wright and Long, of Sydney, but they abandoned it the following year owing to the general mercantile depression, and sold out to Jones.

The working whalers did not find the industry as profitable as did their masters. The rate of pay in 1837 for most of them was three shillings a day and provisions, and in March of that year Jones, Weller and others resisted the demand of the men for an increase to four shillings. Others of the whalers got £12 a tun for the oil, and this was paid in provisions, in clothing, and in rum supplied from the stores of the masters. When it is remembered that the oil was then bringing £40 a tun in the Sydney market, and that in a single season Jones alone shipped no less than 1,800 tuns to that port, some idea of his profits will be gained.

For about eight years the bay whaling industry was one of considerable volume, but, like the deep-sea whaling, it, too, was so vigorously pursued, that the harried whales deserted the coasts of Otago for other shores where they might bring forth their young in peace. That result was foreseen by the astute ' Johnny ' Jones, who acquired

Maori lands and laid other plans to ensure his welfare. But of this more anon.

It was inevitable that in carrying on the shore whaling the Europeans and the Maoris should come into frequent collision, but it must, in fairness, be stated that most of the troubles that arose were provoked by the aggression of the pakehas, who made the native people the victims of their brutality and avarice.

The Maori, before he was touched by Christian influence, never forgot and never forgave an injury. A few instanced may be cited. As far back as 1817 one Captain James Kelly, of Hobart Town, then sailing in the *Sophia*, had killed or wounded some of the Otago natives. For years they awaited an opportunity to avenge the outrage. This came, first, in May 1833, when Kelly, who had had frequent warnings from friendly shipmasters to keep himself and his boats away from Otago, sent a small ship, the *Amity* of 148 tons, commanded by Captain W. Lovett, to these waters. The *Amity* herself escaped capture, but several members of her crew were killed in satisfaction of the old feud.

A similar incident, not without its element of humour, occurred some years earlier at Stewart Island, to a sealing party that had been put ashore. They were unceremoniously killed, cooked and eaten and their stock of provisions appropriated. The provisions included several items unfamiliar to the Maori of the early days. The white dust in the flour bags was used for an amusing pelting match. The soap was sampled until their mouths foamed. Tobacco was chewed and pronounced to be 'heaven's gall.' Some gunpowder was scattered about as useless black seed. Tired of such things, and the savoury ' manfood ' being ready in the ovens, the fires were lit and the feast spread, when suddenly the flying sparks ignited the scattered ' seeds,' and flames of fire leaping among them caused the belief that the gods were making game of them !

In 1834 Captain James Kelly, with more of temerity

than of wisdom, again sent Captain Lovett to Otago, this time in charge of the brig *Mary and Elizabeth*. She only escaped capture by beating a precipitate retreat, but her boat, gear and some dead whales were stolen by the natives.

Three months later a party of Maori warriors on returning from a fruitless war expedition at Cloudy Bay, proceeded to destroy Weller Brothers' station at Otago. This party was headed by Te Whakataupuka, a high chief of the southern territories, who was supported by the Otakou chief Taiaroa. Te Whakataupuka is described as a horrid cannibal ' celebrated as much for his cunning as his courage.' With his marauding force he plundered the houses of the whalers and threatened to murder the whole party. He was only deterred from executing his purpose by the fact that the Wellers, scenting trouble, had persuaded several chiefs to board their vessel, and had carried them to Sydney as hostages for the good behaviour of the tribe, and to ensure the safety of their station. That precaution probably saved the whole whaling gang from being massacred.

It was a curious blend of races and of colours that was drawn into the bay whaling stations, but beneath their divergences of colour and speech and creed, beneath their glories and their shames, their common exultation in the freedom of their life throbbed like the pulse of a true fraternity. There had blown into the bays tough old sea-dogs who would as soon have sailed under the jolly roger as under their own national flags. There were also adventurous spirits who sought in these unfenced regions of society liberty from the limitations of civilized life. There were fugitives from justice, time-expired convicts, and lawless escapees from the penal settlements of Botany Bay and Van Dieman's Land.

Civilization is only a veneer. At its heart human nature is still surprisingly barbaric. With almost fatal facility men relapse, first into barbarism, and then into the savagery from which the race has so slowly emerged. Some

' THINKING OF OTHER DAYS,'

of the poor social outcasts at the bay stations in the lawless days of old ' had never a decent chance in the tangled meshes of circumstance,' and it is not to be wondered at if they abandoned the decencies of civilization, and, without restraint and without concealment, lapsed to a lower level than the heathen in lewdness and in lust.

But the components of the problem were not all of sombre shade. Among the blacks and greys, the ugly mysteries and the uglier facts, ran many a thread of gold. And these worthier factors did bring to some of the dusky children of the New Zealand woods some touch of nobler things than yet they knew, and some knowledge of Diviner things, ere yet the first evangelist had brought his gospel to their shores. Alas, that such light as shone from the better sort of whaler was as but a fleck in an ocean of darkness !

It was a common boast amongst the whalers that there was no law in New Zealand. That applied particularly to the people of darker skin whose wrongs held out small promise of redress. In 1838, at Jones and Palmer's station at Preservation Inlet, a West Indian lad, for the accidental loss of a boat, was mercilessly beaten with a thick spliced rope-end and died in circumstances of the most revolting sort, yet no punishment overtook the guilty parties.

The Rev. James Watkin, the pioneer missionary, whose story will be recited in succeeding chapters, tells in his journal of a tragedy that took place a few months before his arrival, and that for long created great unrest amongst the natives. It appears that on February 15, 1840, a native named Teuteraki Pauwa, son of a petty chief named Pokena, after getting very drunk on a whaler that lay at anchor in Waikouaiti Bay entered the hut of a man named Brown. In a drunken squabble a pane of glass was broken. Part of it struck the Maori, who was deeply incensed and hastily procured a musket. He was taking aim at Brown when a bystander pushed the gun aside. The charge exploded, instantaneously killing a

C

young ship's carpenter. The Europeans were infuriated
and assembled to lynch the luckless man-slayer. Wiser
counsels prevailed and the native and his wife were locked
up under guard with a view of being sent to Sydney for
trial. The feelings of the unfortunate fellow were so
wrought upon by taunts of the hangman's noose awaiting
him, that he begged his white-skinned tormentors to shoot
him. Though in irons he surreptitiously got possession
of a musket, probably from a sentry, and dressing himself
in his best clothes, got his wife to clasp his body from
behind. Putting the muzzle to his breast and pulling the
trigger with his toes, the shot passed through his heart
and into that of his wife, killing them both instantaneously.
The native population was so incensed by the death of
the man's wife that speedy preparations were made for
revenge. Alarmed by the fear of a general rising of the
Maoris, the Europeans induced Dumont D'Urville, the
notable French navigator, who was doing scientific and
survey work in the vicinity from March 30, until April 3,
1840, to give Brown and his wife a passage to the Bay of
Islands.

In the month of March, 1841, during the absence of some
of the Otakou natives to the southward, the French
whaleship, the *Orientel*, which visited the harbour, when
on the point of sailing, kidnapped the wife and child of a
Maori named Taumaita, and the help of the Wesleyan
missionary was sought to secure her recovery, should the
Orientel, as was expected, put in at Akaroa.

These cruel outrages, however, became gradually fewer,
through the influence of the missionary and the extension
to New Zealand of the benefits of an ordered government.
The former of these two forces was at first the mightier,
and even the patriarchal chief, Korako, who will later on
come into this story, paid the missionary the compliment
of declaring in July, 1842, that his advent had put an end
to brutalities towards the native race. In paying this
tribute Korako told an incident that may well close this

chapter, an incident in which he himself had been the
victim. It appears that a blanket was missing and
a search for it had been instituted. Suspicion had
fallen, and not without justice, upon some of the whaling
gang. Their hut was visited by Korako, but before the
bearded old man could make inquiry, one of the whalers
dashed boiling water over him, scalding his face, breast
and side so severely that for ten days he was confined to
his whare. From such a sullied page in that rough island's
story let us now turn to contemplate the conflict that
raged between the Maori tribes of North and South in
the starless night of desolation that reigned before the
arrival of the pioneer prophet of the Prince of Peace.

CHAPTER IV

THE TUSSLE WITH TE RAUPARAHA

If I stoop
Into a dark, tremendous sea of cloud
It is but for a time ; I press God's lamp
Close to my breast—its splendour, soon or late,
Will pierce the gloom : I shall emerge one day.

BROWNING : *Paracelsus*.

FOR long years before the Wesleyan Methodists sent the very first preacher of the ideals of peace and goodwill to evangelize the South Island of New Zealand, the heart of old Te Rauparaha, the famous fighting chief of the North, whose headquarters were at Kapiti, a conspicuous island off Waikanae, was fired with the ambition to invade Te Wai Pounamu. Amongst the manifold motives that stirred the old warrior, two were paramount. He yearned to subdue the pride of the chiefs of the powerful Ngai-Tahu tribe then in possession, and he greatly coveted the stores of greenstone held within their domains. It was not until 1828 that opportunity offered to gratify his longings. In that year he gathered a fleet of canoes, manned them with picked chiefs and fighting men to the number of 300, equipped them with pakeha weapons, and set his course southward. Landing at D'Urville Island his party defeated the residents with great slaughter. Hundreds were killed and eaten and many were sent as slaves to Kapiti. Flushed with victory Te Rauparaha swept the northern parts of the South Island, burning the pas of the Ngai-Tahu, massacring the tribesmen and feasting upon their flesh.

Te Rauparaha was now joined by his famous warrior uncle, Te Pehi Kupe, and in 1829, bent on pushing his way

southward, set off in his canoes on the agreeable enterprise
of wiping out an old insult offered by the tribe at Kaikoura.
Mistaking the visitors for friends the residents invited
them to land, which they did with alacrity, whereupon
the crafty old Te Rauparaha treacherously slew 1,000 of
the unsuspecting Ngai-Tahu, took many prisoners and
celebrated his victory with the customary cannibal orgy.

Shortly afterwards Te Rauparaha was induced to lead
part of his army overland against the Ngai-Tahu stronghold
at Kaiapoi. Under pretence of friendship he sent some
of his leading chiefs into the pa ostensibly for the purpose
of trading. The designs of Te Rauparaha having become
known to Tamaiharanui and other chiefs at Kaiapoi they
struck a decisive and unexpected blow and some eight of
Te Rauparaha's principal lieutenants, who were within
the pa, were slain. These included Te Pehi, who met his
death in a hand-to-hand encounter with Takatahara, a
chiefly warrior who was as fearless as he was strong, and
who first overpowered Te Pehi and then slew him with a
tomahawk.

Smarting under this wound to his pride Te Rauparaha
decided to withdraw to the northward, where, for two
years in his island home at Kapiti, he nursed his resentment
and laid deep schemes for revenge. He set his heart
especially upon Takatahara, the slayer of his uncle, and
upon Tamaiharanui, the chief rangatira of the Ngai-Tahu
tribe, of which he was also high priest and inheritor of
highest ancestral honours, and withal a cruel and ruthless
despot. His dearest wish was to destroy the people of
Kaiapoi and their pa and to compass the death of
Tamaiharanui and Takatahara.

Opportunity was leaden-footed and did not arrive until
late in 1830, when she put in an appearance at Kapiti
in the shape of an armed brig of some 236 tons named the
Elizabeth, commanded by John Stewart, an infamous
villain who was awaiting a cargo of flax for his vessel.
Stewart was inveigled by Te Rauparaha into transporting

the wily old chief and a taua, or war party of 120 Maori braves, including Te Hiko, the son of Te Pehi who had fallen at Kaiapoi, to Akaroa. The force was well armed with muskets and native weapons. The brig arrived at Akaroa early in November, and to disarm all suspicion of the proximity of Maori foes Te Rauparaha concealed his men beneath the hatches of the vessel.

Takatahara, who, it will be remembered, had slain the uncle of Te Rauparaha with his own hand at Kaiapoi, gave an account of subsequent happenings to the Rev. James Watkin when visiting him some ten years later, and these are recorded in the Journal of the missionary, who describes Takatahara as the most powerful, withal the most unassuming chief he had yet seen in New Zealand. Takatahara tells that Te Rauparaha, working through the treacherous Stewart, attempted to allure him on board the *Elizabeth*, but having some suspicion he resisted the overtures. The guile of Stewart, however, was more successful with Tamaiharanui, who was induced to go aboard to trade flax for powder and muskets and blankets.

When Tamaiharanui went aboard the *Elizabeth* he was accompanied by a son, his young daughter and several natives. The party was detained and the old chief put in irons. Later on, two canoes with a number of natives, including the wife of the captive chief, boarded the vessel, never dreaming of treachery. They were promptly put in irons and stowed in the hold. Under cover of darkness, and using the ship's boats and the captured canoes, Te Rauparaha landed with his armed sleuth-hounds, cruelly butchered every man, woman and child save those who escaped to the hills, and then set fire to their whares. Te Rauparaha stood exultant, as, with hands with gore imbrued, he viewed the swarthy glow of leaping flames amidst that wild confusion.

The din
Of groaning victims, and wild cries for life
Proclaimed how well he did his work of strife.

As a new day glimmered on the dying and the dead amidst that scene of desolation preparations were made to cook the bodies of the slain. What flesh could not be consumed was packed into about one hundred baskets and taken to Kapiti that the horrible feast might be continued there. On the way to Kapiti, the captive chief, Tamaiharanui, and his wife strangled their little daughter, named Ngaroimata, lest she should become the slave or the wife of one of his treacherous captors. Most of the prisoners of war were slain and a few were enslaved. Around the neck of Tamaiharanui was hung the head of his son, whose body had been consumed before his eyes. He himself was taken from pa to pa and made the object of derision by his captors, and was afterwards killed by a spear, thrust by the principal widow of Te Pehi, who, with fiendish satisfaction, drank his warm blood as it gushed from the wound. The bodies of Tamaiharanui and his wife were afterwards eaten, the eyes of the fallen chief being swallowed to prevent them, as the natives feared, becoming fixed in the starry firmament.

Te Rauparaha's lust for revenge and bloodshed was still insatiable and his desire to lay waste the pa at Kaiapoi, the scene of his one great and ignominious reverse, became a perfect obsession. A council of war was held with the result that early in 1831 a force of probably 750 braves was mustered. Equipping this war-party with muskets, Te Rauparaha, his blood-revolving breast glowing with sweet anticipation of success, transported them southward. He found the pa at Kaiapoi defended only by a guard of old people, the fighting men, not expecting trouble, having gone to Whangaraupo, in the vicinity of the Lyttelton of to-day, to bid farewell to Taiaroa, the Otakou chief, who, had, with some of his people, been paying a friendly visit to the pa.

The small garrison made such a resistance as quite deceived Te Rauparaha as to the actual feebleness of their forces, and he temporarily retired to consider his plan of action. A siege was decided upon and the investing forces took up their position. Some messengers, eluding the besiegers, carried tidings to the absent members of the tribe. All available forces were hurriedly rallied from neighbouring pas, and, led by Taiaroa, they resolved to raise the siege. Marching under cover of night they approached Kaiapoi to discover that Te Rauparaha's sentries were sleeplessly vigilant. Neither by Te Rauparaha nor by the beleagured garrison was the proximity of Taiaroa's party suspected. At a given signal the relief force broke from concealment with the wild shout : 'Taiaroa to the rescue,' and, leaping into the swamp adjacent to the pa, they were admitted through the wide-swung gate, by those so sadly in need of succour. Systematic plans of defence were now adopted and a battle of wits began that continued for three months with indecisive results.

Te Rauparaha now determined to ' sap ' up to the walls of the pa. At the end of another month trenches had been dug up to within a few feet of the wooden palisades near to which huge piles of dried manuka lay in readiness. The commander of the beseiging party now only awaited a favourable wind to set fire to the enclosure, and for this he had to stand by for several weeks. The defenders saw that disaster was inevitable. Despair looked into their eyes and took possession of their hearts, and thus hastened the day of doom.

Taiaroa resolved upon leaving the doomed pa with his Otakou braves. Under cover of darkness he crept through the swamps at a favourable opportunity thus escaping the ovens of the conquering cannibals.

Meanwhile the hard-pressed garrison reached the heroic resolve to forestall Te Rauparaha by setting fire to the manuka from the inside during a north-westerly wind, hoping that the flames would destroy the piles of brushwood that menaced their wooden defences. A firebrand was thrust into the inflammable mass, at what seemed an

A TYPICAL OLD MAORI.

opportune hour, but unfortunately the wind changed.
Blazing tongues of fire soon doomed the palisades, and
the pa was speedily enveloped in blinding smoke and
devastating flame. Panic seized the luckless defenders.
Such as could not escape were unceremoniously massacred,
irrespective of age or sex, save those only who were reserved
for slavery or for slaughter, as the future necessities of
the victorious Ngatitoa warriors might determine.

This ' bloody deed so desperately dispatched,' by which
Te Rauparaha had achieved his long-deferred and ardently
desired success, only added fuel to the fires of his ambition.
Whilst yet there was rising to Heaven ' the cry of tears
from blackened whares, and of blood from the reeking
earth,' his heart was pondering new plans of pain, and
fresh schemes of slaughter.

Te Rauparaha's star was in the ascendant and whilst it
remained so he would speed the destruction of the hated
Ngai-Tahu. ' Let there be blood,' said he, and soon a
sea was flowing.   Oh, the pity that

> The fiat of this spoiled child of the Night—
> For Day ne'er saw his merits—could decree
> More evil in an hour than thirty bright
> Summers could renovate.

Recalling his former success at Akaroa, a success that
compassed the defeat and death of Tamaiharanui, Te
Rauparaha reflected with bitterness that it yet lacked
completeness as Takatahara, the kinsman of Tamaiharanui
and the slayer of Te Pehi, had been too wily to get within
his clutches. Takatahara, fully expecting that sooner or
later he must fight for his life, had built a strong pa at
Onawe, on a promontory jutting out into Akaroa harbour.
Warned of the projected assault upon his citadel by the
conquerors from Kaiapoi, he was forearmed.

Te Rauparaha, accompanied by many of his Kaiapoi
prisoners, advanced to the gate of the Onawe pa and
began to parley for surrender. Indecision on the part

of the Ngai-Tahu lost them the day, for, whilst Te Rauparaha, surrounded by the Kaiapoi friends of the Onawe people, continued his parley, his own men had gathered and could not be attacked by the Ngai-Tahu without endangering their friends. The sentries at the gate in an unguarded moment allowed some of Te Rauparaha's seasoned veterans to pass within the pa. A sanguinary struggle was speedily decided in favour of the northern invaders. The prisoners were mustered and the more vigorous amongst them marked for slavery ; whilst the aged, the weak and the little children were mercilessly slaughtered. The flotilla of war canoes set out for the north carrying off the prisoners. A few remained behind to repair their canoes. Amongst these was Te Hiko, the son of Te Pehi, into whose custody there had fallen no less a prize than Takatahara who had butchered his father at Kaiapoi several years previously. Te Hiko was a splendid specimen of physical manhood, standing six feet four inches high and well-proportioned. Whilst engaged in repairing his canoe, two women, relatives of Te Rauparaha, demanded Takatahara for the oven. Te Hiko resented this attempt at dictating to one of his high rank, and at interfering with his rights as captor of Takatahara. Curtly refusing the request of the women he put his prisoner under guard, and, with a magnanimity as rare as it was inexplicable in a Maori, he secretly resolved upon Takatahara's release. That night, rousing the late defender of the fallen fortress from his sleep, he took him to the edge of the forest and bade him begone, a behest that, despite his astonishment, he was not slow to obey. Meanwhile the conquerors in their Kapiti stronghold were celebrating their victory in a cannibal orgy.

The Southern Maoris, however, were meditating revenge upon the tribe of the Ngatitoa, and had rallied a party consisting of some 270 toas or braves, under the leadership of Tuhawaiki and Karetai. Hearing that Te Rauparaha was about to visit Lake Grasmere for the purpose of snaring

paradise ducks and other water fowl, Tuhawaiki secreted
his party and awaited the coming of his foe. When the
unsuspecting Te Rauparaha had his canoes beached and
was engaged in setting his snares, Tuhawaiki's men, with
a yell, pounced upon him and he escaped only by precipitate
flight. Such of his men as did not escape with him were
summarily slaughtered. So long as this action was
unavenged Te Rauparaha's reputation was under a cloud,
a condition that he could not brook. He resolved upon
immediate retaliation, and, rallying a war party, set off
in hot pursuit. A sanguinary but indecisive battle was
fought near the mouth of the Flaxbourne River, and the
two parties, each claiming victory, set off for home.
Several months later another expedition was despatched
from the south under Taiaroa. This force, numbering
some 400, encountered Te Rauparaha and a party of his
followers near the head of Queen Charlotte Sound, but,
before any decisive results had been achieved, Taiaroa,
whose commissariat was running low, turned the prows
of his canoes southward.

He was accompanied in this attempt upon Te Rauparaha,
which occurred in the year 1834, by the great Ngai-Tahu
chief, Te Whakataupuka, who was remarkable, amongst
other things, for the possession of six toes on each foot.
Te Whakataupuka had, some two years previously, sold
to one Peter Williams an area of land stretching from the
North Head of Dusky Bay to the South Head of Preservation Inlet, with all the islands between those points,
a transaction that was probably the first conveyance of
land in the South Island. The purchase price of the land
was sixty muskets and these were secured largely with the
hope of using them in revenge upon the redoubtable
Ngatitoa chief, Te Rauparaha.

Disappointed with the result of the northern raid
Te Whakataupuka and Taiaroa relieved their feelings by
attacking various European whaling stations from Cloudy
Bay to Otakou. At the last-named place in September,

1834, they shared in the raid upon Weller Brothers'
station to which reference has already been made. In
the following year Te Whakataupuka disappeared from
Southern Maori history as he then fell a victim to the
epidemic of measles that decimated the native population.
He was succeeded by his handsome nephew, the young
chief Tuhawaiki, who thenceforth became the dominating
figure in Southern Maoridom.

Tuhawaiki was awaiting the opportunity to wreak
vengeance upon Te Rauparaha and his tribe for their
abduction of Tamaiharanui and their numerous other
outrages. But the stars in their courses were fighting
against him. The havoc wrought by the measles epidemic
of 1835 prevented any assault in that year, but plans were
laid for an attack the following year. When everything
was almost ready for the Northern raid a severe epidemic
of influenza, introduced from Australia by ' Johnny '
Jones's schooner, the *Sydney Packet*, took such sad toll of
the natives that warlike preparations were temporarily
suspended.

The section of Te Rauparaha's tribe quartered at Cloudy
Bay formed the determination, early in 1837, to adopt
offensive measures against Tuhawaiki, whose stronghold
was at Ruapuke, and who, since the death of the scoundrelly
Te Whakataupuka, had become the principal rangatira
of the South Island. A taua set out from Cloudy Bay
led by Te Puohu, who, with great daring, travelled overland
with the intention of taking the Southerners by surprise.
After enduring great hardships in the course of their really
wonderful journey, they at length arrived at a kaika at
Tuturau on the banks of the Mataura River. They fell
upon the unsuspecting inhabitants, who were ruthlessly
slaughtered, cooked and eaten. One marauder tore a babe
from its mother's breast and flung it on the glowing coals
before her eyes.

An escapee carried tidings of this disastrous attack
from a new quarter to Tuhawaiki at Ruapuke. He

immediately summoned Karetai, Taiaroa and other chiefs to his aid.   Leaving Ruapuke with his own braves he landed from his canoes at Fortrose. Reinforcements speedily arrived from other kaikas. Concealing themselves by day and marching by night, the party, well armed with muskets, reached Tuturau and found the unwatchful Ngatitoa still feasting on human flesh. A swift blow was struck. Te Puohu, who was a nephew of Te Rauparaha and was accompanied on this enterprise by his two wives, was shot dead by a young chief named Tione Topi Patuki, who cut off the head of the luckless Te Puohu and carried it as a trophy to Ruapuke.   Then followed the historical Tuturau Massacre. Many of the marauders were killed and eaten and some were taken as slaves, including one whose ears were cut off by Tuhawaiki. Topi Patuki, it may be mentioned, subsequently became a native teacher for the Wesleyan Mission. He was baptized by the Rev. Charles Creed on September 15, 1844, and bore a good part in later colonial developments.

But to return. Te Rauparaha was not left long in ignorance of the fate of his invading force, whose extermination stimulated the desire of the Southerners to avenge still further the Akaroa outrage. Throughout 1837 Southern Maoridom was seething with excitement that gave grave cause for alarm to the Europeans at the whaling stations, who were apprehensive for their own safety. In January of the following year Tuhawaiki gathered and equipped five boatloads of warriors.

His summoned prows collect along the coast,
    And great the gathering crews, and great the boast,

as they set out for the region of Cook Straits, in the hope of encountering Te Rauparaha as he returned from a slave raid in Queen Charlotte Sound. Disappointed in this expectation Tuhawaiki returned home with his taua within a month, only to find that once again disease was playing havoc in the Southern kaikas.

In October, 1839, amidst great excitement, Tuhawaiki's final expedition against Te Rauparaha went Northward. It comprised some sixteen sealing and four whaling boats all fully manned and equipped for war.   They reached Little River on Banks' Peninsula on October 30 and found there five Europeans and a boy from Cook's Strait. The party discussed killing the pakehas but were dissuaded by Tuhawaiki, Karetai and Taiaroa, who urged that such action would prevent a visit to Sydney that they were then contemplating.   A compromise was effected by the killing and eating of the Cook Strait boy and a girl of their own company.   The recent years had brought changes in the position and outlook of the Maori people, who were becoming increasingly involved in their relationships with the pakeha.   Te Rauparaha, who had worries enough in the North Island, was now anxious for peace with his hereditary foes in the South, and as the principal Southern chiefs were anxious to visit New South Wales in connexion with certain land sales, a treaty of peace was concluded. Thus ended the age-long antagonism that made it safe henceforth for the tribesmen of the North to visit the southernmost parts of New Zealand.   It was to a land burying a blood-stained past that James Watkin, in May 1840, brought those doctrines of Wesley, that in England, in the eighteenth century, wrought such a moral and spiritual renewal as saved England from the consequences of the operation of forces that for years, across the Channel, wrote the history of France in blood and in tears.

CHAPTER V

THE COMING OF THE PIONEER PREACHER

> I see my way as birds their trackless way—
> I shall arrive ! What time, what circuit first,
> I ask not : but unless God send His hail
> Or blinding fire-balls, sleet, or stifling snow,
> In some time—His good time—I shall arrive :
> He guides me and the bird.
>
> BROWNING : *Paracelsus.*

IT has been said that history is marked by epochs that rise in stately succession all along its far planes, and though these planes are low and shadowed, and characterized by no arresting circumstance, the epochs rise like mountain ranges whose summits are made luminous with the light of upper worlds. At the rise of each epoch there always stands some dominating personality whose gifts so strikingly harmonize with the requirements of the hour that they suggest a Divine ordination to the task of leadership. Such pre-destined correspondence between the moment and the man to match it, affords one explanation of the wonderful unity in history and of the continuity of its great characters. The conjunction of such an epoch and such a personality took place in May 1840, when the Rev. James Watkin, the first herald of the Cross in the South Island, pierced the dark horizon of Otago history like a veritable shaft of light and unfurled the subduing flag of Jesus Christ on the incarnadined soil of the southern regions of Ao-tea-roa. This harbinger of a new day came to New Zealand just when Time was tolling the mid-night hour of Southern Maoridom, and when the blight of whalers' wickedness had deepened the gloom in which tribal war and the crumbling of their ancient faith had enveloped the dusky dwellers of the district. An old epoch was dying and a new was waiting to be born. Mr. Watkin attended at its birth and by his contribution at that critical epoch founded a new order in the life and history of the province.

The story of the circumstances that led to the appointment of Mr. Watkin deserves to be put on record. The English Wesleyan Conference which had, since 1822, been engaged in mission work amongst the North Island Maoris, designated Mr. Watkin for work at Kapiti at its sessions in 1839. Kapiti and Otaki were, by mutual consent of the Anglicans and Wesleyan Methodists, and with the approval of their governing bodies in England, in the Wesleyan sphere of influence. In breach of the existing compact an Anglican clergyman, twenty-three years of age, and then in deacon's orders, was sent to Otaki. This young man was the Rev. Octavius Hadfield, to whom reference will be made in a subsequent chapter dealing at length with the fraternal unity with which the two Churches met the challenge of a hateful heathenism.

In 1839 the Wesleyan Missionary Society had already decided to evangelize the South Island of New Zealand, hitherto untouched by Christian enterprise. When the Rev. J. H. Bumby, who was the Superintendent of the Wesleyan Mission in New Zealand, heard that Mr. Hadfield had intruded into the Wesleyan sphere and occupied a station for which Mr. Watkin had already been designated, he, with fine Christian spirit, resolved upon a re-arrangement of the Wesleyan appointments so as to avoid unhealthy rivalry and wasteful over-lapping. Early in 1840 Mr. Bumby visited Sydney to confer with the Missionary Committee at that place. The Committee resolved to appoint the Rev. Samuel Ironside, then labouring in the Hokianga station, to open up at Cloudy Bay in the South Island. It was still deliberating as to whether a second

THE HOBART TOWN WHALING SHIP, DERWENT HUNTER.

South Island station should be opened at Banks Peninsula
or at Waikouaiti when Mr. Bumby was approached by
Mr. ' Johnny ' Jones, the owner of a whaling station and the
claimant to extensive Maori lands at Waikouaiti. Mr.
Jones made an offer which he later committed to writing,
and the original letter now lies before the writer. It reads
as follows :—

Sydney,
January 29, 1840.

Rev. Sir,

In reference to the establishment of a Mission by the
Wesleyan Missionary Society at my station at Waikawat,
I beg to say that I am very anxious to afford every encouragement in my power towards such an undertaking, and
agree to afford a missionary and his family a free passage
to the Station in one of my ships, to give a suitable piece
of land for the use of the Mission, to send the Missionaries
supplies from time to time free of any charge, and shall
present to the Society towards the expenses of this Mission
a Donation of £50.

I am, Rev. Sir,
Yours faithfully,
John Jones.

To Rev'd. J. H. Bumby,
   Chairman of the New Zealand District.

It may be observed that Mr. Jones broke almost every
clause of his undertaking, but his letter led Mr. Bumby,
without further consultation with his committee, to select
Waikouaiti as the headquarters for work by Mr. Watkin.
The Rev. Samuel Ironside did not begin his work at
Cloudy Bay until December 1840, hence to Mr. Watkin,
freed by the action of the Anglicans from his original
appointment, fell the distinguished privilege and honour
of inaugurating the first Christian Mission in the South
Island of New Zealand.

Arrangements were made for Mr. Watkin and his family
to sail from Sydney for Waikouaiti by the little brig
Magnet in March 1840, but as this vessel registered only

D

148 tons and was carrying a group of paheka passengers for the agricultural settlement of the ship-owner at Matainaka, and five Maori chiefs who had been negotiating with Governor Gipps for the sale of their lands, as well as some twenty head of cattle and supplies of provisions, it was determined to defer the departure of the missionary until the month of May. Passages were booked by the *Regia*, a little teak-built brig of 180 tons gross register, which had been built five years previously at Cochin, Malabar Coast, Madras.

On Friday, May 1, 1840, the *Regia* left her anchorage in Sydney and crept quietly down the harbour for the port at Waikouaiti. The blue waters glistened in the sunlight. Birds made insolent music in the foliage of venerable gum and wattle trees that then graced the site of future Sydney suburbs. The smoke of the straggling city rose in the rear, whilst seaward the skyline was broken by grassy slopes and rocky headlands. It was a scene, full, at once, of rugged grandeur and of exquisite grace. As the occasion was one of historic interest it will repay us to take a closer scrutiny of the brig and her company.

Two boats drawn by a towline followed in the wake of the *Regia*. One was intended to take back to the city the friends of departing passengers who had received permission to accompany them down the harbour. The other was to carry home the pilot when he had safely taken the brig beyond the Heads. A few groups were gathered on the little vessel. Her owner, Mr. ' Johnny ' Jones, was standing with his wife, engaged in quiet conversation with the pilot and Captain Kyle, the commander of the brig.

Four clergymen, the Revs. W. Schofield, J. McKenny, Webb and Weiss, were looking into the earnest face of a Methodist missionary, short of stature yet strong of feature. It was the Rev. James Watkin, who, two years and seven months previously had come to Sydney after spending seven years evangelizing the heathen of Tonga.

Seated on the closed hatchways, her face bearing traces of life and motherhood in the tropics, was the young wife of the missionary. A baby, not yet eleven months old, sat upon her knee. Before her stood her little girl of five summers holding the hand of a brother scarcely two years her junior. Several Methodist women, Mesdames Iredale, Orton, Weiss and Matthews, were speaking words of love and cheer to Mrs. Watkin, who gazed wistfully towards the city that had lately been her home—the only English home she had known since, ten years before, as a new-made bride, she left England for missionary work beneath the Southern Cross.

Two other of the missionary's sons, the senior not yet nine and the junior a little over seven years old, stood at the stern with a youth named Matthews and several of the Jones children, watching the sportive gulls and recounting with animation their childish memories of Tonga and their anticipations concerning life amongst the Maoris.

Suddenly there was a general movement. The various groups converged and the cadences of song floated softly over the placid waters as they sang Dr. Watts' hymn as revised by John Wesley,

> Come ye that love the Lord,
> And let your joys be known.

When the melody had died away one of the ministers lifted his voice in prayer and commended the travellers to the care of God—

> Who rides upon the stormy sky
> And calms the roaring seas.

The visitors took an affecting farewell of the voyagers, and as their boat drew away gave three ringing cheers, which were returned by the ship's company. Soon the Heads were passed, the pilot dropped, and the only passengers—the family of the missionary, and one whom Mr. Watkin described as ' a young man of amiable manners '—were left gazing at the receding shore. This young man was a Mr. William Morgan, junior, son of a Sydney merchant, who was paying a short visit to New Zealand.

A few hours later as the sun sank westward amid a perfect riot of crimson and gold, and the stars began to stud the heavens, and the shades of night to shroud the land, the missionary was thinking long thoughts that skirted alike the islands of memory and the mist-girt continent he had left behind. At nightfall he gathered his family for worship in their cramped quarters. It is doubtful if at any altar beneath the Southern skies that night there assembled any family that outshone in gifts of brain and heart the bright galaxy that gathered in the little cabin of the *Regia*. If one had then possessed power to cast the horoscope he would have foreseen for each a bright future. The father and three of his sons each won elevation to the Presidential chair of Methodist Conferences, whilst the mother and daughter and remaining son, in other spheres, all won distinction. But that is another story.

The first night at sea the little brig, rolling in rhythmic response to the swell of the ocean, caused severe discomfort to the passengers, whilst the sheep, cattle and horses that constituted the chief part of her freight, suffered sadly from the close confinement. Day after day, for ten dreary days, the sluggish little vessel tacked and veered as fair winds alternated with buffeting breezes and tantalising calms. Only once was the monotony of the voyage broken by the sight of a sail on the horizon and that too far distant to be ' spoken.'

The eleventh night at sea was one of storms, and, as the captain had not previously visited the Southern parts of New Zealand and anticipated picking up the coast at any hour, it was a time of some considerable anxiety and for a good part of the night the brig was ' hove to.'

At about five o'clock on the morning of May 12, in

the dark before the dawn, the look-out man discerned a
light ahead. Thinking it might be a light on shore, the
captain was aroused, and the ship put about with no small
noise. The light proved to be the Morning Star shining
through the murk. It was at once a herald of the coming
of day and a prophet of the vanishment of the night of
wrong that shrouded this island before the missionary
had bid the gloom-encircled Maori ' lift his gaze on high
to see the glory of the glowing sky.'

An hour later as the advancing day began to ' dapple
the drowsy east with spots of grey,' and to furrow all the
orient into gold, Solander Island was sighted, cutting the
horizon some nine or ten miles on the weather bow. They
entered Foveaux Straits, through which they must pass,
before a staggering breeze, but ere the passage was cleared
the wind died away, and as the *Regia* broke the fretted
waters with a tenuous trail of foam, new perils confronted
her. The captain, hoping to clear all danger, kept his
boat well to the eastward, and thereby ran into dangers
that threatened him with disaster. By ten o'clock island
after island appeared in alarming proximity. Wind there
was none, the canvas flapped idly, and the *Regia*, at the
mercy of the current, was in extremest jeopardy. As
the little ship with her living freight was drifted past these
perils, and into the rugged region of Waipapapa Point and
Slope Point, the appalling sound of breakers, like deep-
toned thunder, grated on their ears, and the heavy set of
the swell, gripping the tiny hull, was driving her towards
the dread Otara Reef, over which rolled the remorseless
seas that have there buried many a ship's company in an
unmarked and indiscriminate grave. When destruction
seemed imminent, a little breeze sprang up, the ship was
hauled a few points off shore, out of the heaving of the
terrific surf and at a safe distance from the rocks.

Progress, however, was still impeded by alternations
of contrary winds and of dead calms, during which latter
the currents carried the *Regia* on her course. It was not

until the night of May 15 that she made Waikouaiti Bay and dropped anchor in that exposed harbour.

No landing could be effected before morning, but ere the night was far advanced a strong wind blew in fearful gusts that soon stiffened to a gale, and transformed the bay into a tumbling, racing sheet of wind-tossed water. The little brig reeled before the onslaught of the waves as they smote her sides and gurgled along her deck. The wild wind shrieked through the cordage, the canvas cracked like cannon, the masts creaked, the booms tugged at the blocks, the rudder banged from side to side, the hull groaned, and so great was the strain upon the anchor that, at about ten o'clock, the chain parted. The dashing of the rain, the hissing of the water and the roaring of the wind, combined with the thunder of the breakers to leeward as the vessel made stern way, were terrifying in the extreme. With as much expedition as possible a second anchor was let go and all the chain that could be given it, some ninety fathoms, was paid out, with but slight hopes that the brig would, by its aid, mock the fury of the night and ride until the morning. There confronted the storm-tossed travellers the meloncholy prospect of being again compelled to put to sea, should such a thing prove possible, or of being driven ashore with the certainty of being dashed in pieces. About midnight, however, the tempestuous wind mercifully moderated, and though it continued to blow hard all night, the chain held until the morning.

With the dawn of Saturday, May 16, 1840, the Rev. James Watkin, then in his thirty-fifth year, had his first view of the scene of his future labours, and about noon he, his wife and five little children, planted their feet on the shining sands of Ohinetemoa, the name by which the beach of Waikouaiti Bay was known in ancient Maoridom. To this land the missionary had come, not for wealth, honour or conquest, not in search of adventure or in pursuit of knowledge, but swayed by the dictates of duty and moved by the constraint of love.

Subsequent chapters will tell the stirring story of what he dared and how he fared, of what he sought and how he wrought, when he embarked upon the adventure of life and labour in a land just emerging from savagery, an adventure in which he was certain of nothing save of the guidance and guardianship of God, and of the purpose and the power of the Gospel he preached to uplift and redeem alike the brown-faced dwellers of Ao-tea-roa and the pakeha denizens of those then unfenced regions of society.

Chapter VI

THE HERALD OF A HIGHER RACE

One who never turned his back, but marched breast forward,
   Never doubted clouds would break ;
Never dreamed, though right were worsted, wrong would
   triumph ;
   Held we fall to rise, are baffled to fight better,
              Sleep to wake.
                    Browning.

The first little cluster of Otago's real settlers preceded the coming of the pioneer missionary by only a few weeks, and in that tiny group of colonists James Watkin read the prophecy of a stream of new and better blood flowing to the coasts of Maoriland. With a clear vision of the potentialities of the place he saw that the loftiest destiny of the land could only be fulfilled as its foundations were laid in righteousness. Hence he set himself the task, not only of redeeming the Maori from heathenism ; of purifying the soiled lives of pakehas who had lapsed into the barbarism that stands mid-way between civilization and savagery ; and of subduing the recalcitrant forces of the community, but also the task of exalting the ideals and uplifting the aspirations of the newer settlers, so as to permeate the nascent commonwealth with the moral ideals of the kingdom of his Divine Master.

James Watkin's contribution to the early life of Otago, a contribution that began before British sovereignty was established in that region, has become part of the country's heritage. Deprived of the rich endowment of his self-forgetting service, Otago would have begun its career

THE HOBART TOWN WHALESHIP, *PACIFIC*.

of colonization tragically deficient in the elements that contribute to national well-being. His work and that of the Rev. Charles Creed who succeeded him in 1844 paved the path for the Scottish settlers of 1848, and did much to create the conditions that made possible the acquirement and peaceful occupancy of treasured tribal lands by the sturdy sons of Scotia. The person of such a pioneer of Providence will always be invested with interest, hence it may be well to place on record what the literature of the land at present lacks—an authentic biographical sketch of the man who first brought to that southern isle the undimming radiance of the religion of the Lord Christ.

Born in Manchester, England, on September 29, 1805, and enjoying the advantages of upbringing in a godly Methodist home, James Watkin was converted in early life and soon felt the call to devote himself to the Christian ministry. He commenced to preach in the Oldham Street circuit in his native city, and there was privileged to enjoy the ministry of the Revs. Jabez Bunting and Richard Watson, two brilliant Methodist preachers whose efforts were acknowledged by Wilberforce to have contributed largely to the abolition of the slave trade in 1807 and to the success of the famous petition to the House of Commons that resulted, in 1833, in the emancipation of the West Indian slaves. A gentleman of means, impressed by Watkin's native talent, offered to pay the whole cost of a University education at Oxford if he would take holy orders in the Church of England. This offer was rejected, and in the year 1830 he was accepted as a candidate for the Wesleyan Methodist ministry.

Mr. Watkin offered for service in the foreign mission field and felt drawn to India. The missionary committee, in view of the needs of its far-flung activities, debated about sending him either to Stockholm or to Mauritius. Suddenly the dancing needle of his life's compass, moving at the impulse of energies beyond human guessing, swung to the South Pacific. One of three men designated for the

Friendly Islands was unable to go and Mr. Watkin was appointed to accompany the Revs. Peter Turner and William Woon to the Tongan group, with his special location at Tongataboo. Prior to leaving for the mission field he was ordained at Sloane Terrace Chapel, Chelsea, and was married in London on June 30, 1830, to Miss Hannah Entwisle, a niece of that saintly and distinguished Wesleyan minister, the Rev. Joseph Entwisle. The ancestors of Mrs. Watkin had come to England with William the Norman. One had fought at Agincourt and was killed in the first battle of the Wars of the Roses. Other forbears linked her with the royal house of the Stuarts and with that brilliant ecclesiastic, Edward Irving.

Mr. Watkin with his wife and his colleagues left Gravesend in the whaling ship *Lloyd's*, owned by a Quaker merchant, on August 7, 1830, and after a voyage of five dreary months reached the Bay of Islands in the north of New Zealand on January 7, 1831. Here they were left on shore while the ship made a short whaling cruise. After this pleasant break the voyage was resumed and they reached the Friendly Islands on March 10, 1831, to find the group ablaze with the fire of religious revival.

Some thirty years previously Tonga had experienced its baptism of blood when the agents of the London Missionary Society were murdered. Now the labours of the Wesleyan missionaries, the Revs. Walter Lawry, John Thomas, Nathaniel Turner and William Cross were bearing fruit, and island after island was renouncing idolatry. Mr. Watkin saw and shared in the revival in which thousands were converted from savagery, and heathen worship was swept away. At Haabai he saw one of the most remarkable revivals of modern times. In a few weeks thousands were added to the Church. An immense sanctuary was erected for him at Lifuka and here and else-where he preached from pulpits whose stairs were adorned with disused war clubs, and administered the sacred emblems at altars, the communion rails of which were fashioned from carved spear shafts surrendered by erstwhile savage warriors.

The influence of Mr. Watkin operated greatly in the revival in which there was converted the famous Taufa-ahau, who subsequently became the King of the whole Tongan group, and who, until his death on February 17, 1863, proved himself, by wise and beneficent rule, one of the ablest native rulers of modern times. The code of law he promulgated in 1839 brought the Friendly Islands into the circle of Christian nations. Taufa-ahau proved himself ' very mischievous to the gods ' and soon the sky was darkened with the smoke of idol-consuming fires. Angered by the success of the ' lotu ' some of the older chiefs attacked the Christians at Nukualofa in the Tongatabu group. The missionary families and the printing press were removed for safety to Vavau and James Watkin returned alone, and, facing the fury of heathen hate, secured a footing in the very fortress of these chiefly foes to the faith. Taufa-ahau, grateful for the work of Watkin, wrote in August 1836 to the Rev. Joseph Entwisle, expressing thanks that he had spared his kindred to bring light to Tonga. He said that formerly ' he had stuck to heathen evils like pitch, and was plastered all over with sin.' Now he rejoiced that heathen worship was destroyed, their former deities disowned, and their idols cast to the bats and the moles.

In the midst of this great revival the Tongan missionaries heard the wail of the strangled Fijian widow and the throb of the death-drum of the cannibal temple, and seizing upon Watkin's facile pen his colleagues directed him to appeal to British Methodism on behalf of fierce Fiji. In burning words he wrote his message and gathered up his pleas into the poignant and compelling entreaty, ' Pity, oh Pity, Cannibal Fiji.' This cry from a heart anguish-stricken at the horrors of unbridled cannibalism, was published in 1838. Its message rang with signal effect.

It immediately stirred the heart of British Methodism to its depths and aroused a quenchless interest in Fiji. An immediate result of its publication was the dedication to the cause of evangelizing these ferocious cannibals, of the lives of those eminent missionaries—John Hunt and James Calvert. The tract did much, too, to bring about the annexation of Fiji by the British Government. Incidentally, a German translation of the appeal led Mr. J. F. H. Wohlers to dedicate his life to the missionary cause, a life that for long years was lived in the interests of the Southern Maoris.

For nearly seven years Mr. Watkin was associated with the Tongan people. Throughout the group he was spoken of as ' the man who knew everybody.' With the native teachers he went to remote villages, and with them, too, he sailed the seas, as with consummate skill, they navigated their double canoes through the stormy and reef-strewn Polynesian waters. Often he was in peril of the sea, in perils of the wilderness and in peril among the heathen. Troubles had to be met and war had to be encountered. Possessing a natural aptitude for languages, Mr. Watkin speedily acquired fluency as a Tongese preacher. The greatest native Tongan orator of his generation, the Rev. Apollos Mau Mau, said that no foreigner ever equalled Mr. Watkin as a speaker in that tongue. As a translator of Scripture and a writer of hymns he did good work, and possessing an insatiable thirst for knowledge he soon became recognized as a living encyclopœdia on all matters relating to the Friendly Islands.

On September 11, 1837, with his wife and the four children born to them in Tonga, Mr. Watkin set sail for Sydney in the brigantine *Minerva*, commanded by Captain Milne, a South Sea Island trader. On the way to Sydney they touched at the Bay of Islands, where a week was spent, the trip from Tonga to Port Jackson occupying thirty-nine days. In Sydney, Mr. Watkin's eloquent preaching brought him into prominence with the English colonists, amongst whom he exercised a ministry of great and growing influence for two years and seven months. Whilst in Sydney he often preached in the open air, taking his stand in the Domain, or in the locality then known as ' The Rocks,' or on the foundations that were then being laid for the York Street Wesleyan church, which for long years after stood in the very heart of Sydney as the cathedral of Australasian Methodism, an altogether imposing pile of massive masonry with its graceful sweep of stone steps and impressive Corinthian colonnade, a sanctuary whose walls in after years often resounded to his voice.

Of his work in New Zealand it is only necessary here to say that the Maoris soon came to look upon Mr. Watkin as their protector from vicious and avaricious whites, and by reason of his boundless zeal and wide learning he came to be known amongst the natives as ' the little man of great energy and wonderful knowledge.'

There was about James Watkin that subtle something that men call ' personality,' and that touch of genius that pen portraiture always fails to catch. He was an omnivorous reader with a good mental digestion and a remarkable capacity for absorbing knowledge. His life-long friend, the Rev. Samuel Ironside, whom the present writer knew in his maturest years, and with whom Mr. Watkin maintained a correspondence for forty years, says that the subject of this sketch was the best-informed man he had ever met. His letters were rich in information and showed striking versatility. They sparkled with wit and humour, with shrewd comments on passing events, descriptions of persons met with, and criticisms of books read. His sermons were thrilling, heart-searching, soul-converting, and in the pulpit and on the platform his humour sparkled with effectiveness. He had a bright and ready wit and a gift of keen and pungent satire. These were, however, well governed by sound sense and softened by gracious benevolence and instinctive Christian kindliness. He was a ready writer, a willing worker, a faithful pastor, a generous friend, the uncompromising foe of hypocrisy, but as free from malice as a babe. Self-disparagement was characteristic of him, yet not even his severest critic could say of James Watkin what was said of St. Paul, that ' his bodily presence was weak and his speech contemptible.'

The Journal kept by Mr. Watkin during the turbulent times he spent at Waikouaiti from 1840 to 1844 reflects, as no other records can do, the conditions of Otago in the pre-settlement days. The pages show how he trod the highway of love and found it not always a flower-strewn path, but often a rough road that lacerated the feet of the traveller. He had a heavy load to lift, acutest agonies to endure, fiercest temptations to face. Despite it all he put up a record of duty done, difficulties met, dangers passed and triumphs won of which any one might well be proud, and when, in June 1844, he left for Wellington by the *Deborah*, that also carried the surveyors who had been in quest of a site for the establishment of a Presbyterian Free Church Settlement in days yet far distant, he bequeathed to posterity a splendid possession. A future, newly born and rich with promise, was displacing the old order of savagery and lawlessness. The Maoris had seen a shining ideal. The pakehas were thinking bigger thoughts. Racial unity was finding some recognition. Men with white faces and brown were becoming interested in each other's welfare and a new atmosphere had been created. He had tramped what truly seemed a treadmill round, but found at length that it had in reality been a spiral up which he had led the feet of many a new disciple.

His subsequent story does not come within the scope of this volume and may be told in barest outline. Transferred to Wellington he exercised a profitable ministry to people of both races, and there he was often consulted by Sir George Grey, who placed a high value upon his advice in the perplexing problems affecting the relations of the Maori and pakeha. In the year 1855 Mr. Watkin was transferred to New South Wales, and seven years later, at Adelaide, was elected President of the Wesleyan Methodist Conference of Australasia. In 1869 he retired from active ministerial work, but spent the years of his superannuation in useful Christian service until physical infirmity kept him within his own home at Ashfield, a suburb of Sydney. At the age of seventy-eight, he, with his son, the Rev. W. J. Watkin, suffered shipwreck when the steamer *New England* was lost on the bar of the Clarence River, an experience that left its mark upon his constitution. Shortly before his course ended, he had the joy, on March 17, 1886, of seeing his whole family beneath his roof for the first time for thirty-four years. The assembly included six sons, two daughters, and thirty other relatives who had come to honour the old veteran and his wife, who for fifty-six years had sustained a happy partnership. On May 14, 1886, at his little cottage that bore the name ' Waikouaiti,' he passed away in the eighty-first year of his age and the fifty-sixth of his ministry, with the words of the Apostolic Benediction loitering upon his lips. His body rests in the Rookwood Cemetery in New South Wales, within a few yards of the grave of the Rev. Charles Creed, the first minister who ever preached in Dunedin, and who for the eight fateful years between 1844 and 1852 sustained and developed the work throughout Otago and beyond its borders that Mr. Watkin had so well begun.

Chapter VII

BRITISH BEGINNINGS AND PAKEHA PASSIONS

All that we glory in was once a dream,
The World-Will marches onward gleam by gleam,
New voices speak, dead paths begin to stir,
Man is emerging from the sepulchre !
Let no man dare, Let no man ever dare
To mark on Time's great way : ' No Thoroughfare.'

Up till the year 1840 the South Island of New Zealand was little known to the outside world, and concerning it the very haziest ideas prevailed. Fourteen years earlier Captain James Herd of the *Rosanna* passed up the East Coast after calling at Stewart Island. He was in quest of a site for settlement, but saw nothing to encourage such an enterprise and relinquished the idea. A few years later several small parties of whalers and sealers were to be found scattered at isolated spots along the coastline. New Zealand itself had not come under British sovereignty at the dawn of 1840. The New Zealand Company was then anticipating landing the first batch of immigrants at Port Nicholson. There was no Settlement at Nelson, nor had the projects for establishing an Anglican Settlement in Canterbury, and a Presbyterian Free Church Settlement in Otago yet come out of the clouds. Within the boundaries of the South Island no civilized code of law had yet begun to operate.

In the year 1837 a petition had been sent by missionaries and other settlers in the North Island praying King William IV to extend to New Zealand the blessings of British government. That petition served to speed up

TE RAUPARAHA,
An Old Maori Warrior.

the land sharks in Sydney and their confreres in New Zealand in their inglorious task of dispossessing the Maori of his landed inheritance. The total area of New Zealand is only about sixty-six million acres and an index to pakeha cupidity is given in the circumstance that eight claimants to Maori lands demanded no less than 56,594,000 acres, chiefly paid for, so they alleged, in such currency as muskets, powder, bullets, tomahawks, tobacco, blankets and rum. At Otakou alone an aggregate area of 5,018,200 acres was claimed. Weller Brothers advanced a claim for 3,560,000 acres in various localities. For this they had given a consideration of £153. 'Johnny' Jones contented himself with a claim to a paltry 1,980,000 acres.

Early in 1840 such parts of New Zealand as were, or might be, acquired for the British Crown, were added to the boundaries of New South Wales and placed under the control of Governor Gipps and his Legislature. Captain William Hobson, R.N., was appointed as Lieutenant-Governor and at once left Sydney for the Bay of Islands. A Proclamation, dated January 14, 1840, was issued relating to this enlargement of the boundaries of New South Wales and the appointment of Captain Hobson. Another Proclamation was issued affecting land acquired from the natives. This declared that the Crown would not acknowledge the validity of any title to New Zealand lands save those ' derived from, or confirmed by a grant to be made in Her Majesty's name.' It further provided that no owner would be dispossessed of land purchased on equitable conditions, and that a Commission would be set up for the consideration of all such matters.

Tuhawaiki, Karetai and three minor chiefs were then in Sydney. From these men Jones and Weller had acquired large areas of land and were now seeking to use the natives in their own interests. The chiefs waited upon Governor Gipps on January 31, 1840. The representative of Her Majesty at once saw that the chiefs were being used to pull the chestnuts of the land buyers out of the fire,

E

and scorned the suggestion of the said buyers that the recently-issued Proclamation was ' an insult to the chiefs ' who had sold them the lands. The Governor told the chiefs that he could not confirm their past land sales and then sought their consent to the Proclamation of British Sovereignty. They agreed and undertook to sign a Deed to that effect. In consideration of that undertaking the Governor, according to the official papers still in existence, gave ten guineas to each of them, and arranged for them to sign the document when it was ready. While it was being prepared, however, Mr. W. C. Wentworth, ' Johnny ' Jones and a number of others arranged to purchase from these chiefs and their fellow-chiefs in New Zealand, the whole of the South Island and some 200,000 acres in the North Island, subject, however, to certain sales already made. For these multiplied millions of acres they paid the chiefs £200 and promised each an annuity of £100. Thus ' got at,' Tuhawaiki and his four fellows refused to fulfil their promise to sign the Governor's Deed. Though temporarily outwitted the Governor had not long to wait to turn the tables on the skilful and wily conspirators.

The five chiefs returned to New Zealand in the *Magnet* in March, with the first batch of settlers for ' Johnny ' Jones's station at Matainaka, and there awaited the turn of events. Whilst so waiting there arrived in Otago Harbour, on March 30, 1840, Dumont D'Urville, the notable French navigator, who, in prosecution of scientific research in the Pacific, was in command of an expedition in the vessels *Astrolabe* and *Zeleé*. They spent four days in Otago waters, and it is worthy of mention that the artist with the expedition has preserved to posterity two glimpses of Otago in those far-off days. One of these pictures shows the parai, or beach nearly opposite the Spit, and the other gives a view in the vicinity of the Maori Kaik. Special interest attaches to one picture as it gives the only representation extant of an Otago double canoe of that particular period. Other interesting features depicted are the rude huts and the high food stages, or ' fateo ' as the Otago Maori called them, on which can be seen the bodies and tails of a couple of drying sharks. D'Urville passed northward on April 3, and recorded a most unflattering description of the natives and also of the whalers, who, he said, ' led a life of indolence and disorder, abandoning all their work to their native women, without whom they confessed they could not live.'

On May 16, six weeks after the departure of D'Urville, Mr. Watkin, as we have seen, landed at Waikouaiti. Five days after the coming of Watkin, Lieutenant-Governor Hobson issued a Proclamation asserting British Sovereignty, but that Sovereignty was not finally proclaimed until the following month. The celebrated Treaty of Waitangi was in process of signature by the North Island chiefs when Mr. Watkin was making his first acquaintance with Southern Maoridom. Following up the steps he was taking to ensure British Sovereignty, Governor Hobson had despatched Her Majesty's ship *Herald*, in command of Captain Nias, to the South Island. After touching at Akaroa she went to Stewart Island, where the British flag was hoisted. Passing to Ruapuke on June 9, the moko, or copy of his facial tattoo marks, was secured from Tuhawaiki for the Treaty, which was also signed by Taiaroa. The signatures were taken by Major Bunbury, for whom Mr. E. M. Williams acted as interpreter. The *Herald* came to Otago Harbour on June 13, where Karetai, who, like Tuhawaiki, had given Governor Gipps a refusal of his consent to the proclamation of British Sovereignty, now also signed the Treaty without demur, as did also Korako and other chiefs. After securing these signatures the *Herald* passed on to Cloudy Bay, having first paid her respects to two French and to two American whaling vessels then in Otago harbour. This courtesy over, the American captains crossed in a whaleboat to Waikouaiti for the purpose of attending religious worship with Mr. Watkin the following day, which was Sunday, June 14. In the morning they courteously rowed him across to his Matainaka service and in the afternoon joined in worship at Waikouaiti, the *Herald* meanwhile speeding on her mission. Upon arriving at Cloudy Bay, a Union Jack was hoisted at the pa of Horahora-kakahu on June 17, 1840, and a royal salute of twenty-one guns was fired, thundering forth to the world the declaration that New Zealand was now under British Sovereignty and a part of the colony of New South Wales.

The ratification of the Treaty of Waitangi by the chiefs— a result largely secured through the persuasion of Tamati Waaka Nene, the head of the Ngatihao tribe and a member of the Wesleyan Church—gave the British Government power to set up established authority in New Zealand and to control colonization and other vital matters in the interests alike of the Maori and the pakeha. To the Maoris, the Treaty guaranteed full and undoubted possession of their lands, estates, forests, fisheries and other properties. It conceded to the Crown the exclusive right of pre-emption over such lands as the natives might wish to alienate, and gave guarantee of Royal protection to the natives, who, by the Treaty, enjoy the rights and privileges of British citizenship. In his Journal, Mr. Watkin recorded gratification at this consummation and expressed the hope that British law might be brought into operation for the protection of the natives and for the suppression of the enormities practised by the Europeans.

Sydney now became the nominal seat of constituted authority, and so it remained until May 3, 1841, when New Zealand became a separate colony with Captain Hobson as Governor. The New South Wales capital was, however, too distant for effective control, and on February 15, 1841, Mr. Watkin recorded his fear that unless the Government effectively interposed, the South Island Maoris would soon be regarded as intruders on their own soil, especially in those parts most valuable to themselves, namely the river mouths and harbours. For the time being Mr. Watkin stood alone in the South Island as the representative of constituted authority, and a bitter price he paid for his solitariness. In course of time the Commission set up by Governor Gipps made inquiry into the land purchases that were questioned, and made its awards. How it did its work may be judged from the simple fact that ' Johnny ' Jones and others were dispossessed of large areas too cheaply acquired, and that the Waikouaiti station owner was awarded 2,560 acres out of the 1,980,000 that he claimed to have purchased.

In the light of later events one can but marvel at the crass stupidity and imperious pride of the Europeans who refused to enter the mind of the coloured man and to look at things from his standpoint. Not only was the Maori cheated out of his tribal inheritance by avaricious speculators and by greedy land companies, such as that, which, as Mr. Lindsay Buick graphically says, afterwards wrote its faithlessness in letters of blood on the floor of the Wairau valley ; but he was defrauded in trade by unscrupulous ship-masters, and grossest outrages were ruthlessly perpetrated by many a pakeha villain. In these things lay, to a great extent, the roots of the Maori rebellion, and of the long and bitter struggle for native rights that drenched the land with blood in the racial wars of 1860–1870. One such outrage that was visited by speedy retribution, but not upon the actual culprit, took place in March 1840 whilst Tuhawaiki was on his way home from Sydney. One John McGregor visited Ruapuke in a thirty-ton schooner he had built, and kidnapped several slaves, three men and three women, belonging to a chief named Robulla. He departed leaving one of his own men ashore. When he learned of his loss the chief was infuriated, and with about fifty of his men armed with tomahawks, seized the poor unfortunate, and despite the pleas of the victim to be spared until the return of Tuhawaiki from Sydney, he was immediately

chopped in pieces and devoured. So keen were the
frenzied cannibals upon vengeance that they did not take
time even to strip the miserable wretch of his clothes.

Upon coming to Waikouaiti, Mr. Watkin found himself
in conflict with the elementary passions of man at his
vilest. The vicious and unclean habits of the white man
had been grafted upon and mingled with the original
heathenism of the aboriginal inhabitant. Brutality and
licentiousness abounded amongst the whalers, by whom
abominable vices were publicly practised. These men
were almost generally living with native women. They
looked suspiciously upon the advent of the missionary
and bitterly resented his efforts to extirpate this vile
traffic in virtue. Some prevented their women, or as they
vulgarly called them, their ' heifers,' from attending either
school or church, well knowing that if the Christian religion
gained an influence over the native mind, they must either
marry or lose their concubines upon whom some had come
to rely for their own sustenance. Often these men treated
their partners most cruelly, and one, within a very short
period, had laid three of his illicit lovers beneath the sod.
The Rev. Samuel Ironside, known to the Maori as Te
Haeana, tells that at Port Underwood, late in 1840, the
services of Maori girls were hired by the whalers for a
season for half a keg of rum or of tobacco. The position
was scarcely better within the sphere of Mr. Watkin, for
he records with disgust that native parents gave to visiting
whalers for the paltriest consideration a season's use of
' girls of so tender an age that they had not yet developed
a single sign of puberty.' Against such things he never
ceased to struggle, although often his rebukes of the
haunting shapes of sin seemed like sand thrown against
the wind.

In Otago in 1840, evil was not a negative thing. It
was a positive, militant, destructive energy. It defied
the resources of law and of civilization. Selfish greed,
degraded passion, colossal crime and diabolical cruelty

hurled their challenge at the prophet of a new order. That challenge he was not slow to accept. But his was not a conflict merely to destroy abounding vices. It was a constructive conflict undertaken to reform character, to re-make men and to re-fashion the conditions of life alike for the Maori and the pakeha. The cost of that campaign in heroisms, risks, toils and sorrows, ere yet he saw some fruitage of his holy warfare, no arithmetic can calculate.

Mr. Watkin knew—indeed few knew better—the frailty of human nature at its strongest and its best, and his understanding heart was stirred as he looked upon these men whose life story was like a torn and tattered manuscript. In base surroundings the brute had become predominant and man's intrinsic glory was suppressed and hidden. Virtue had been scorched in the fierce fires of temptation. Battered ideals strewed the trampled track of life, and the tragedy of their ruin was heightened by their own acquiescence in it, and by the hopelessness of their despair. But ere these men could be healed they must be wounded. Over their path 'fiery passions had poured their wrath in hurried desolation,' and on the fields of their lust Maori maidens lay broken like ruined temples. Little wonder that these whites winced under the lash of Watkin's stern rebukes, which brought their sins into the daylight like ghosts out of the gloom. Well he knew, as he swung his Master's whip about wrong-doing, that he had planted his feet on a path that led to Gethsemane, but beyond that place of agony he saw the vision of white men, aided by a Power vaster than the whole sea of circumstance, gaining victory over the forces that thwart and hinder, damage and degrade ; and yet another vision of a duskier race escaping alike from the grave-clothes of heathen vices and the fetters of pakeha devilry.

It was but natural that the hate of the evil-doers should focus itself upon the man who dared to condemn their sin. His very presence, as he moved among them in white armour, pierced like a stiletto to the centre of soul and conscience. Their resentment showed itself in various ways. Sometimes the ribald laughter and vile execrations of drunk and devil-possessed men beat upon his brain like a veritable devil's tattoo, and at others a dour silence, more eloquent than speech, was the manifestation of their malevolence. But Mr. Watkin never despaired of them. He knew that the Gospel he preached had in it a power to redeem the lapsed, the low, and the lost, and to renew the sin-soiled in Christlikeness. His heart, aching like a torn wound, yearned to know that their sins were covered with the merciful veil of Divine forgiveness and forgetfulness. He sought to stimulate a moral sense that had confused the very principles of morality, and that had ceased to register the decrees of conscience or to feel any recoil from the horrors of sin. He strove to bring them a vitalizing breath of heavenly air. He told them they need not make a final surrender to evil, that life still had a meaning for them, that even yet the tomb of dead ideals might be the womb of living purposes, and there was a wideness in God's mercy like the wideness of the sea, and that, through Divine grace, they might even then let

> The sulphurous rifts of passion and woe
> Lie deep 'neath a silence pure and smooth
> Like burnt-out craters healed with snow.

Personal wrongs done to Mr. Watkin found little space either in the pages of his Journal or in the ledgers of his memory. A few casual Journal entries, however, reveal the life of the period and are therefore worthy of note. There died at Waikouaiti on July 1, 1842, a native woman of some thirty-five years, named Tautaki. Her death had important results alike for pakeha and for Maori. In the case of the latter it was truly historic as it led to the virtual abandonment of that burden on the native race—

A MAORI WAR CANOE.

the law of tapu. Tautaki's husband, influenced by Christian sentiment, dared to break from every sacred custom of his fathers. He refused to remove the sick woman to an outhouse and leave her to her fate to ensure that the living might not be inconvenienced by the dying or the dead. He did not refrain from using his hands in eating. He refused to tie up his wife's dead body in an old blanket and to throw it into the customary hole two feet deep, but arranged for a deep grave to be dug in the homori, or cemetery, and there the wife was interred on Sunday, July 3, in accordance with the rites of the Church. The melody in the pioneer preacher's heart at this sign of conquest was marred by a protest ' like a note that jars the music in the sweet flow of a song.' It so happened that Tautaki's grave was near to that of Mrs. Thomas, the wife of the Superintendent of Mr. J. Jones's station, who had been buried the previous Tuesday, and whose husband, within a few short days, was to be laid by her side. The Europeans were furious at the burial of a native in a plot adjacent to the grave of a pakeha, regarding it as a blow against the superiority of the white race. At his evening service, after the interment of Tautaki, Mr. Watkin frankly told the objectors, with unflinching plainness of speech, that if any superiority existed it belonged to the natives and not to themselves. Some of the objectors were Australians, but most were Americans, and these the missionary further scarified by referring to their vaunted Declaration of Rights—' All men are free and equal '—and then asserted that in whatever country it had been his lot to live, he had ever found them the most virulent enemies of their dark-skinned brothers.

Whilst the whites were still smarting under Mr. Watkin's words, death was busy gleaning his harvest and the missionary was again called upon to officiate at the burial of a man who had died in the horrors of a drink-induced delirium. Most of the Europeans attended the funeral,

at which Mr. Watkin gave a short address in the course
of which he referred to the evils of alcoholic indulgence.
He told how drink dissipated their earnings, brought them
to wretched poverty and shortened the span of life. He
reminded them that the previous October three boats had
been wrecked and that six out of the eight of those who
lost their lives were drowned whilst drunk. He showed
how morally indefensible was the practice that sapped their
vital forces, debauched their manhood, devastated the
hearts of their women and despoiled the lives of innocent
children. After pleading for an abandonment of their
drinking habits the service came to an end amid a hush
that was broken only by the deep-toned thunders of the
ocean

> Echoing far through the moaning air,
> Like the distant chant of a wild despair.

An hour later, going down to the store, Watkin found a
number of men in an advanced stage of drunkenness.
His plea for sobriety had not enhanced his popularity,
and finding himself the subject of renewed execrations
he wrote, ' Their blame must be my praise. I should
suspect myself if I had their encomiums.'

The day following this event Mr. ' Johnny ' Jones sought
the help of Mr. Watkin, the only disinterested and competent person near at hand, to straighten out a tangle of
business affairs caused by ' unprincipled persons who had
been preying upon him.' Although the task was foreign
to his office and he was well aware that his action would
gain for him added ill-will, he felt he dare not, by refusing,
' give tacit sanction to further imposition upon Mr. Jones,'
who had, by the way, done little for him. The same
week Mr. Watkin had also to interfere in a case of brutal
violence perpetrated by a white man upon a native boy,
and the gloom of these dark days was deepened by the
serious illness of his wife, as well as by threats of personal

revenge. But the dauntless stoicism of the man is manifest when, notified by disgruntled whites that they will boycott his services for his plain speaking and prevent their concubines attending, he makes the laconic comment—'the viper and the file.'

The lawlessness and deeds of violence in Otago in the days before the 'Settlement,' were, as in our own day, mainly attributable to the use of alcoholic liquor, as is apparent from what Mr. Watkin wrote in his Journal on September 3, 1842 :

'The state of things here is alarming. Property is insecure and life scarcely more so. Robberies have been rather numerous lately and two nights ago Mr. Jones's store at this place was broken open and robbed. I have dwelt among people called savages and amidst war's alarms, but never felt such a painful sense of insecurity as I do at this place. Things are nearly as bad as they can be. Love of strong drink appears to me the source of most of the evil here.'

Amidst such dismaying difficulties, the Wesleyan pioneer did his work with dauntless spirit and with tireless industry. He rendered a service without which the moral foundations of the Province would have been sadly defective, and created elements that contributed greatly to peaceful settlement and to stable national life. The spiritual results are beyond defining. They baffle both speech and arithmetic. To attempt an analysis is to shame one's pen by poverty of words. James Watkin created a new atmosphere and you cannot define an aitmosphere any more than you can fathom mother-love.

CHAPTER VIII

GAMESOME GODS AND CARICATURES OF DEITY

Like the tides on crescent sea-beach
When the moon is new and thin,
Into our hearts high feelings
Come welling and surging in—
They come from that mystic Ocean
Whose rim no foot hath trod,
Some of us call it *longing*,
We know that it is *GOD*.
—Professor Carruth.

Upon his arrival at Waikouaiti the Rev. James Watkin found the religion of the Maori a medley of notions and forms and fears emptied of any spiritual meaning they may once have possessed. The ancient Maori cosmogony had in it many elements of grandeur and not a few points of contact with the Jewish stories of Creation. The old tohungas, or tohukas, to use the Otago form of the word, used to tell that ages and ages of Nothing, and uncounted æons of Chaos and primeval Darkness preceded the appearance of the Heavens and the Earth, and also ante-dated the birth of Light from which there gradually evolved the Ao-marama, or World of Light, in which at the fulness of time there took place the Dawn of Life. Io, the Supreme God and the first great Cause in the Maori theologic system, was well-known to the priests, although they did not, at any rate in later times, pass on this know-ledge to the common people, in whose affairs Io consequently did not count as a factor.

The Southern Maori of 1840 was adrift rudderless on seas unknown and uncharted. Kahukura, the patron deity of the Ngai-Tahu tribe, and all the old gods, had failed to vindicate their worth at the bar of human experience. Traditions about the gods were still cherished but, apart from the heritage of dreads and fears of uncounted legions of deities, the flames of an ancient heathen faith were fast flickering to extinction. The Maori had suffered spiritual disillusionment and had been shocked into doubting the truth of old ideals and the virtue of old forces. Such an hour in the evolution of any people is always an hour of crisis and that hour found the Otago natives in parlous plight. They did retain, however, a slavish faith in the power of the priest and under his domination their lives were largely lived.

The tohungas preserved and passed on to their sons the old cosmogonies, the mythology relating to gods and to heroes, their racial genealogies and their treasured tribal traditions. Into these stories of race and of religion, with all the mysteries of occult and esoteric lore, the priests initiated the taula and other grades of the learners of folk-lore and the like, and to them also they imparted instruction in the sacred arts of carving and of tattooing. It was the priest who revealed to the people hidden things. He interpreted their dreams and their omens. It was he who often practised makutu, or the exercise of the black art; he who afforded protection against witchcraft and the evil eye. It was he who healed diseases by repeating chants to appease the wrath of angry atuas and he who summoned spirits to his aid. He, alone, could grant absolution from the dread law of tapu, and it was he who presented the offerings to the gods.

Shortly after his arrival Mr. Watkin records conversations that he had with Kurakura, a chief of the Ngati-huirapa hapu of the Ngai-Tahu tribe, who was also known as 'Wrymouth' from a facial contortion that disfigured him, and also with a patriarchal chief and priest named

Korako. The subject of the conversations was the immortality of the soul and the future life. These conversations disclosed a belief in the reality of the spirit world and somewhat nebulous notions about a hereafter. Ancestor worship was a constituent of their religion and they imagined that the dead could hurt them and bring ill or good luck. To gain the goodwill of the spirits and to charm away the threatenings of the skies they honoured the spirits by offering sacrifices, human and otherwise.

Korako, who had an exceptional knowledge of Maori lore, said that the location of the future life was a place called Tauamotu and that thither his spirit would repair when dislodged from his body. The body would be left behind to be burned. Upon the arrival of his spirit at Tauamotu it would furnish itself with a new body by washing in the wai ora, or water of life that is found there. In that state the reclothed spirit would live in much the same fashion as here, save that it would have more to eat and less to do, ' a Paradise,' says Mr. Watkin, ' sufficient in the estimation of a Maori.' Pointing to his own shadow cast by the morning sun, old Korako declared that the shadow was the soul that would live. Angrily resenting the suggestion that his shadow was a mere consequence of natural causes he reiterated his assertion that it was his soul.

' Well,' said Mr. Watkin, ' everything that casts a shadow must have a soul. My house there, that cask, and this— ' as he picked up a stick and raised it so as to cast its shadow. The idea of ' the soul of a stick ' was too much for Korako's temper and his anger blazed, whereupon he was told that anger is not good, and it was a poor cause that had to be supported by such means. Korako's anger did not prevent him developing a liking for visiting the Mission House, but he confessed to Mr. Watkin that his atua was very incensed with him for doing so. The displeasure of his god did not greatly interfere with the paying of frequent calls upon the ' mihinari ' (missionary).

The Maori had more gods than were ever known on the
Acropolis. In 1840 the land seemed to possess fewer men
than gods within its coasts. One old Waikouaiti chief,
holding up his outstretched hands and repeating the word
'ten' over and over again, said there were 'plenty tens'
of deities. The Maori was a born mystic. He believed
that all natural objects and all phenomena are possessed
of a wairua, or indwelling spirit. He was a Nature-
worshipper and saw personality in all created things.
From the nadir to the zenith the Universe was peopled
with spirits. His life, from the cradle to the grave, was
haunted with ghostly presences. Nature was 'a sybil
with a thousand tongues,' though the tongues spoke with
little of the tones of tenderness.

Time and space, earth and sky, sunlight and shadow,
winds and rain, birds and beasts, trees and stones, life
and death, misfortune and loss, mental processes and
acquired knowledge—all were personalised and deified.
The edible rhizome of the bracken fern was personified as
'Haumia.' The pounamu, or greenstone, prized by every
Maori and from which he laboriously fashioned the mere
and the tiki and other weapons and ornaments, was
endowed with sentient faculties. The quivering of the
heated summer air was the dancing of Tane-rore, the child
of Hine-Raumati, the beautiful Maiden of Summer. The
rainbow was the outshining of Te Aniwaniwa. The
atmospheric phenomenon of a fog and all the different
phases of Nature were regarded as the production of the
gods. Lightnings were the dread arrows of an angry atua.
Thunder and the raging of a storm were outbursts of
offended deities. Flood and fire as well as defeat and
disaster, disease and death were all caused by spirits of
evil. Every peril of the Maori was personalised. Foes
and famine, storms and suffering, blighting pestilence,
rainless skies, failing crops, all had behind them a
'personality' that needed to be cajoled or otherwise
conciliated.

The Maori never dreamed that he lived in an ordered world. He knew nothing of the unvarying action of the laws of Nature, those fixed habits of a beneficent Deity. Nature afforded no guarantee that she would hold to a uniform course. At any moment she might deviate capriciously from her established line of movement. He knew nought of the kindly significance of a Universe that to him, as to us, is yet full of mystery. His was a religion without hope and without comfort. No spirit of benevolence quivered in its life, nor did any god of gladness give a genial smile. ' Storm and darkness in their mingling might ' spoke only of dread presences. The Maori lived on the brink of calamity, for ever apprehensive. Taniwhas and monsters inhabited sea and land, enchanted trees and demon-haunted rocks and many another peril threatened him, by day and by night.

The interests of the Maori were circumscribed. His needs were few and simple. He wanted food and fellowship, shelter and security. He sought for little of comfort to-day, and thought still less about the needs of to-morrow. But when the thought of to-morrow did obtrude it put a tension upon his nerves. He was then a victim of vexing thoughts and rankling doubts and of fears that made his life a gloomy prison house. He was a mere shuttlecock of capricious sprites, or the sport of mischievous deities. His days were filled with fear, danger and uncanny adventure. The fancied presence of the unseen met him at each step of his pilgrimage. Every hill and cave, every stream and lake, every plant and tree was possessed of a spirit who was as variable in his moods and tenses as he was ill-disposed in his nature.

It is little wonder that this ' child of a thousand chances ' lived under a ceaseless tyranny. He felt that his fate lay in the hands of hostile powers, who had to be bribed and placated in order to secure at their hands protection, safety, happiness or victory. To appease or to outwit the spirits who controlled the forces of Nature that were

REV. JAMES WATKIN.

so inimical to man's interests was his unending task. The dreads and dangers of the dark appalled him and he feared to be alone. The dark was a great abyss inhabited by fearsome presences. Each cave was a lair wherein lived ghosts and goblins. Man-devouring spirits dwelt in tapued buildings. The atua, ever malign and vindictive, exercised a ceaseless, prying domination over his doings. He spilt their brimming joy-cups, spoilt their plans, entangled their nets, overturned their canoes, gnawed at the vitals of the sick. Scarcely more fearsome than these gods of the ancient Maori, were those tormenting devils of whom Dante tells, and whom Charles Lamb describes as ' tearing, mangling, choking, stifling demons.' They did something more than fit the phrase of Wordsworth—' a wild brood of gamesome deities.' They were beings of the more sinister sort pictured by Pope—

> Gods partial, changeful, passionate, unjust,
> Whose attributes were rage, revenge and lust.

The disappearance of any former elements of loftiness in their old religion, and their belief in such gods as now the common people knew, had, in the Otago of 1840, induced among the natives a servile, slavish fear that bit like acid into the finer qualities of character, marring the personality and robbing the Maori of his true heritage. Religion was then, in Southern New Zealand, a chaos of dark superstitions, interlaced with which was the law of tapu. The operation of that law was both a burden and a curse, and the natives fancied the lightest infraction of the tapu would be visited by certain death. To break down the power of the tapu Mr. Watkin at once bent his energies. He deliberately broke the tapu and denounced it as both false and foolish, and asked the natives why the gods did not kill him. They somewhat shame-facedly replied, ' Our gods can only kill Maoris.' Upon one occasion at Waikouaiti two priests were greatly incensed

F

at his action in describing the law of tapu as the fruit
either of ignorance or of fraud. They tauntingly asked
him to prove the superiority of his religion by raising
the dead to life. He replied that it was no part of his
profession to raise the dead, but that his Master would
do that in His own good time. His teaching even sooner
than he had expected, proved fatal to the tapu in Southern
Maoridom. In another chapter is related the story of
how that ancient tyranny received its death-blow in
connexion with the decease of Tautaki. With this
passing of the tapu, there also perished for ever in these
southern regions the power and the prestige of the
priesthood.

Among the strange superstitions held by the Waikouaiti
natives was the belief that cripples belong to a superior
class, and should a cripple approach a common fire it
would involve instant death to those gathered around.
Superstitions of another sort speedily gained ground.
Mr. Watkin tells that on October 15, 1840, he saw and
conversed with a native who had returned from the Bay
of Islands, and who professed to possess a puka kakari,
or war book. These books were supposed by the Maoris
to operate as a most potent charm. If carried on the
person in time of war or combat these mascots would
render the possessor invulnerable alike to the bullets
and the clubs of the enemy. Moreover, a shot fired by
the fortunate owner of a paku kakari would always hit
the mark, and the bullet would glance from one to the other
of the victims intended to be struck by it, until ten had
fallen to a single shot ! The natives had been led to believe
that Mr. Watkin had such books but was sedulously
keeping them from the Maoris. The missionary declared
that he possessed no such books nor were any such in
existence.

' But I have one myself,' said the native from the North.

' And you say that if you are shot at, you cannot be
wounded ? ' asked Mr. Watkin.

' I cannot,' asserted the Maori.

Being near the doorway of the mission house and an empty fowling-piece lying close at hand, Mr. Watkin quietly made as though he would try the experiment, whereupon the native owner of the magical volume, to the immense amusement of the missionary and all beholders, cried out in alarm ' Kati, kati,' which being interpreted means ' Don't, don't.'

The story of the discredited native passed on to Otakou Heads where Bishop Pompallier was paying a flying visit a few weeks later. The Roman Catholic prelate, who himself was credited with possessing miraculous powers, has put on record his own version of the fabulous puka kakari.

Many strange notions got afloat in those days of old, mainly through the agency of half-instructed natives, and some amusing attempts were made to graft some novel growth upon the Christian stock. In November 1840 some Waikouaiti natives brought to that place a puka tapu, or sacred book, to which wonderful virtues were ascribed. It was said that if one of these books was placed upon the chest of a dead person he would be at once raised to life. Mr. Watkin asked to see this wonder-working volume, which turned out to be a copy of Norie's *Epitome*. When he apprised the natives of the nature of the book those who had proclaimed its efficacy were greatly ridiculed for giving credence to such a fable.

A ringing challenge to assail the citadels of superstition was flung out by the facts confronting the missionary. He saw the darkness of mind induced by the curse of polytheism, by the withering influence of priestcraft, and by the blight of haunting fears, and was not slow to make his onslaught. Mr. Watkin well knew that the battle would be grim, stiff, relentless. Yet beyond its smoke he already saw the light of victory gleaming, and he knew that when heathenism had spent its strength the hosts of Jehovah would still be singing their morning melody to magnify the sovereign grace of God who sits upon the throne.

The old faith of the Maori was inadequate to meet his deep, though inarticulate need. It gave no satisfying knowledge of the Supreme, no power to overcome sin, no peace for the fainting soul, no certain knowledge about the future. Debased ideas had made every thought of God a nightmare. He was a Being in whom were but aggravated the defects of their own character. Mr. Watkin's supreme task was to give the Southern natives new thoughts of Deity. To these ignorant people he brought many a beautiful chalice of thought from which they drank to their souls' refreshing. He sought to lay hold upon any worthy elements in their old faith and to find any substratum of truth underlying their manifold errors. Such things, representing the mere alphabet of infant minds, he used to introduce them to richer resources of spiritual knowledge.

But whilst he led them with gracious gentleness to larger truth, he did not hesitate to wound that he might heal, to destroy that he might rebuild on fairer lines. He showed the sheer stupidity of Nature-worship. One day, pointing to a whale that had just been captured and lay dead upon the beach, he said, ' It is a pretty god that can be killed.' But, as he lay bare the utter irrationality of their old religion, he showed them in clearer vision, behind the face of Nature, the Supreme Personality whom they ignorantly worshipped. He gave to them their first conception of an ordered Universe in which there operated laws that did hold to an undeviating course, a conception that in time slew their superstitions and banished their fears of capricious forces. He revised their blurred notions and corrected their caricatures of the Almighty. God was not vindictive, nor did he delight in damning men, in blasting innocent joys or in snatching away the things that delight men most. Such a notion, he taught the Maori, was an atrocious slander upon the

Divine character. God did not stand apart in colossal calm, coldly sublime, indissolubly just. He was not too high for their upreaching, nor was he deaf to their beseeching. He was a Father who loved His Maori children and embraced men of every race, and men of every hue in one great family.

Such teaching it was, in the early forties of the nineteenth century, that led the Otago natives, who before had seen only terror and darkness lurking around, to hear the call of the All-Father, and to lose their fears in his all-embracing love. The ancient atuas had been weighed in the balances and found wanting, and as the true God entered with a brighter dawn, the false gods passed for ever into a darker night. In their new relationship as sons of God the Maoris found safety, supply, satisfaction, and amidst the glow of this new knowledge there melted away the dread of to-day and the tyranny of to-morrow.

The religion of the missionary met these terrorized children of the night with a message of hope. It brought light to their darkness, power to their feebleness, healing for their hurts, redemption from their sin. It created a new moral character in a people foul with the vices of heathenism. It met also the invading paganism of the pakeha whaler, and in the case alike of the brown man and the white, it uplifted them to virtue and inspired them to goodness. Incidentally, too, it operated to create the conditions for colonization, when, in the unfolding years the hour should strike for the commencement of the Scottish pilgrimage that has brought so much of blessing to Southern New Zealand.

Chapter IX

'HAUNTING SHAPES OF HORROR'

Through many a dark and dreary vale
They passed, and many a region dolorous,
A universe of death . . .
Where all life dies, death lives and Nature breeds
Perverse, all monstrous, all prodigious things,
Abominable, inutterable, and worse
Than fables yet have feigned or fear conceived.
—Milton.

THE spread of Christianity amongst the Maoris of the North Island had not been without its effect even to the remotest South. The spirit of the gospel, about which they yet knew so little, had commenced to wear down the forces of a foul and savage heathenism which had reeked with human sacrifices and with cannibal orgies. Raw savagery was no longer openly practiced and the sounds of tribal wars were being stilled when Watkin began the first effort to win South Island Maoridom for Christ. The younger generation of natives was feeling the impact of European civilization as exhibited in the lives of rough whalers, of escapees from the penal settlements in Botany Bay and Van Dieman's Land, and of other outcasts from ordered society. The older generation of barbarous, bone-picking cannibals had, however, not yet passed away. There still lived many who bitterly resented the intrusion of the pakeha, who resolutely resisted the influence of the missionary and who were rebellious at the proposal to establish British sovereignty in Ao-tea-roa.

Long indulgence in the practice of cannibalism had, in a measure, dehumanised the older natives. They had accustomed themselves, at their ghastly feasts, to gorge with gusto and without revulsion on stinking and putrifying flesh. Early in 1837 some of those amongst whom Watkin worked a few years later had joined the taua, or war party, which perpetrated the bloody massacre at Tuturau, near Mataura, and then had cooked and eaten the flesh of their victims. Many a time these men had exchanged with friendly tribes the flesh of fallen foes. This flesh they had partly preserved in air-tight baskets made of flax or in containers made of kelp and encased in the bark of the totara tree.

An outstanding figure of the old school was Korako, one of the most aged Maoris in the country. He belonged to the Kaiterakifakabito hapu of his tribe, which had its quarters at Waikouaiti. In addition to holding the office of chief he wielded great influence as a priest or tohunga. The face of the old man bore the furrows of time as well as the marks of the tattooing instrument. Korako remembered, in his young manhood, the visit of Captain Cook, and treasured for many years a tomahawk given him by the great navigator. With this tomahawk he had been wont to instil terror in the hearts of his enemies. Not a few fell to his prowess. After chopping their heads open with his hatchet Korako would, with his strong, wiry fingers, tear out the hearts of his fallen foes, and while yet the hot blood was flowing would devour them so that the valour of the victims might become incorporated with his own.

Korako himself had not escaped scatheless and he bore the marks of many a wound received in stern encounter. Out of his rich resources the old man loved to talk with Watkin about the language, customs, experiences and religious beliefs of his people, although he protested that his atua, or god, was angry with him for visiting the mission house. On June 4, 1843, Korako told Mr. Watkin that his coming to Waikouaiti had put a final end to cannibalism, murder and other evils that were formerly frequent.

It is worthy of note that Korako, under the guidance of the Rev. Charles Creed, professed a desire to renounce heathenism and to forsake the evils of priestcraft. As a chief he was, however, a purua, or a possessor of two wives. One, named Hamiria, was a young girl, the other was the aged partner of his early manhood. Korako was told that a condition of reception into the fellowship of the Christian Church was that he must be the husband of one wife. To his credit be it said that he elected to stand by Kupukupu, the companion of long years. Both were baptized and also married according to Christian usages on July 19, 1848. The patriarchal old chief and quondam tohunga chose as his baptismal name Te Wakena (Watkin) and his wife the name Mata Wakena (Mother Watkin). The old couple witnessed a good confession for the remainder of their days. Korako himself received Christian burial at Waikouaiti on November 3, 1852.

For long centuries before the advent of the white man the Maoris had been accustomed to offer human sacrifices. Their gods were real to them and as terrible as they were real. They were assumed to delight in bloody offerings. The lives of slaves were ever at the mercy of their masters and many a slave was sacrificed by the worshipper from sheer cruelty and love of bloodshed. Sometimes the body was cooked between two burning logs and then eaten, not so much to satisfy hunger as to ensure that the strength of the victim would pass into the votary.

Human sacrifices were offered, too, from the best of motives. The only deities the Maoris knew were capricious beings. Of such they lived in constant fear. Every misfortune was interpreted as the malevolent action of some god who needed to be conciliated. This necessity to restore the god to good humour set the strings of sacrificial instinct vibrating. The Maori could conceive

TAMATI WAAKA NENE.

CAPTAIN HOBSON, R.N.

Fathers of the Treaty of Waitangi.

of no more costly sacrifice than human life. He imagined that the blood of men would be likeliest to gain from the gods life for the lost and mercy for the living. On other occasions a human sacrifice was offered merely to provide a dish for a ritual feast or to give éclat to a tribal function.

Very early in his career at Waikouaiti, James Watkin had to deal with a threatened recrudescence of the practice of offering a human sacrifice. The nearest neighbour of the missionary was Kurakura, alias Wrymouth, a notable chief who belonged to the Ngatihuirapa hapu of the Ngai-Tahu tribe. He was a venturesome canoeist and had often courted disaster in the face of warning and of entreaty. One day, accompanied by his wife and daughter, his brother's wife, a nephew and three others, he left Waikouaiti by boat for a place to the northward where some of his people were engaged in flax cutting. At the very spot whither they were bound, the mast, the sail and the nose of their boat drifted ashore. A catastrophe had happened, the cause of which must ever remain a mystery, for not one of the nine unfortunates survived to recite the reason of the tragic ending to their excursion.

Tidings of the disaster were brought to Waikouaiti, and on the night of March 4, 1841, Mr. Watkin was startled by an agonising cry of many voices. It was a bitter wail of hopeless grief which is ever the saddest of sounds that breaks upon the human ear. Hurriedly descending the hill to the Maori kaika, the missionary was told of the drowning of Kurakura and his company and beheld such a sight of misery as one may never forget. Korako, the aged chief and priest who had, by the disaster, lost his only two sons, a daughter-in-law and a grandchild, was rolling on the ground in a paroxysm of despairing grief. Parents, relatives and friends of those who had found a watery grave were wailing in their misery.

While the mourners were yet in the throes of grief word reached Mr. Watkin that some natives had resolved to offer as a human sacrifice to the manes of the departed chief a slave who had been taken prisoner in one of the wars with the Northerners. Taking with him Mr. W. G. Thomas, Superintendent of ' Johnny ' Jones's station, Watkin hurriedly sought out the natives involved in the matter and told them he was aware of their intention. He pointed out the wickedness and the futility of the procedure and warned them that such an act was contrary to British law under which they had lived since the previous June. He also held over them the threat of a murder trial and the certainty of death by hanging for any one who slew for sacrifice the chosen victim whose name he announced. Moved by the emotion of the missionary, the patriarchal old Korako, broken by grief and heart-hungry for his lost loved ones, gave his assurance that no such sacrifice would be offered. Addressing Mr. Watkin another declared, ' Since we have heard you say " Thou shalt not kill " we are afraid of doing the things we used to do.'

Kurakura and some of his ill-fated companions had been amongst the best and most promising of Watkin's scholars, and the missionary took the opportunity to tell the mourning Maoris that he had brought to them the gospel of a single and sufficient sacrifice for all men. He told also that God did not demand sacrifices from man in order to gain Divine goodwill. Such goodwill already existed and had been shown in the gift of God's Son, who fulfilled all the sacrificial practice of mankind and who was, both to Maori and pakeha, all and more than all that they had meant their victim to be.

Often the heart of Watkin was stirred at the hopeless grief of the Maoris in the presence of death. Their religion had in it no power to transmute sorrow into a sacrament. In the burial ground near to the mission house Mr. Watkin often saw one Maori father, with his head wrapped in a blanket, come so that he might sit and weep beside the grave of his dead son. Another native used to wear as an ear pendant the jaw bone of a favourite child—a touching token of his tender feeling.

The Maoris held the belief that the spirits of the departed used to take their flight to Te Reinga, a spot near Cape Maria Van Dieman, and thence to plunge into the sea as the portal to paradise.

In the days before the advent of the missionary it was not uncommon for a widow to strangle herself so that her spirit might accompany that of her husband as he took his flight to heavenly habitations.

One native widow woman who had grasped the idea of the Christian hope of a re-union never to be broken, used to seat herself in the late afternoon on the brow of Hautekapakapa Hill, near the mission house. As she watched the setting sun her thoughts would circle about her departed mate and her heart hunger would voice itself in the lament called a ' waiata tangi ' :

> Kua mate toku hoa, hua riro,
> Ekore ia e hoki mai ki,
> Au-ei-e-ie ;

the interpretation of which is :

> My companion is dead, he is gone,
> Never will he return to me,
> Alas ! Alas ! Alas !

Sometimes her lament would take the following form :

> Kua riro taku hoa,
> Ekore ia e hokiki,
> Au-kei te pouri toku ngakau-
> Aianei ha haere au-ki-a-ia.

This may be translated :

> My companion is gone,
> Never again will he come to me.
> My heart is sorrowful,
> But soon I shall go to him.

Such laments were a feature of the poetic expression of the Maoris.

Until the coming of the missionary the Christian estimate of the sacredness of child life was unknown to the Southern Maori. The practice of romi, or infanticide, was tragically common, and was operating to hasten the extinction of the race. Watkin did his best to eradicate the horrible practice. Unwanted infants were sometimes destroyed simply to escape inconvenience. They were not often killed by violence but were abandoned to the wild pigs or left to die in lonely places. Amongst the young, unchastity was prevalent, and the fruits of illicit unions were treated like unwanted kittens. Cases have been known where a jealous mother has killed her little one simply to spite a father who loved his child too well. Sometimes children were killed for fear that their cry might betray to an enemy the presence of those whom they meant to attack. Not infrequently the innocents were slaughtered to prevent them being captured and brought up in slavery.

Watkin tells of a young wahine in his mission school—Roihi Whatirauwhea by name—who at her birth had been doomed to death by her unnatural mother. This woman had dug a hole in the ground, thrown the child in, and hurriedly covered the little one with loose earth. Being only imperfectly buried the child cried out lustily and was rescued by neighbours from a living grave. It is sad to relate that in early womanhood Roihi succumbed to the enticements of a whaler and became his concubine. She fell ill and was visited by Mr. Watkin. Being satisfied with her profession of faith the missionary baptized her on September 10, 1843. Fifteen days later, at the age of twenty-three, this crushed flower was laid to rest in the native cemetery. The service was conducted partly in Maori and partly in English, and the missionary records that her pakeha paramour appeared a good deal affected by her death.

As late as July 1841 Mr. Watkin met with a case of infanticide, and he records that the foul deed was perpetrated by a mother whom he describes as being, without exception, the most forbidding female he ever saw.

Gradually the Maoris learned the worth of the child, but, like their white-skinned fellows, only slowly have they come to recognize that the function of the parent is to shape these plastic personalities in self-control, mould them in moral beauty and fashion them in Christ-likeness of character. Such a purpose can only be achieved as parents guard their children from every vice that would blast the fair promise of their lives and smite the pestilences that threaten to sap their physical force, arrest their mental growth or palsy their moral attainment.

The moods and tenses of the tattooed children of the woods were variable and chameleonic. They were creatures of caprice controlled less by reason than by a succession of emotional despotisms. They had been cradled in a gory bed and nurtured in a wild and bloody world. The blood-lust, so deep-seated in human nature, and proclaiming so loudly the ancestry of the jungle, rioted within them. War had been their pastime, and the practice of seeking utu, or revenge, for real or fancied wrongs, led to many a sanguinary battle. The missionary often had difficulty in restraining the natives from acts of bloodshed in which they delighted to engage on the slightest provocation.

Mr. Watkin tells that very shortly before his own arrival at Waikouaiti, a great warrior named Kahu (the Hawk), who had performed surprising feats of valour, had, in the very hour of death, been raised on his mat and supported in a sitting posture to give his final advice to his tribe. He lamented that he was dying a mean death in his house instead of an honourable death in the fight, but he charged them when he had gone to the clouds to avenge his death upon their enemies. Kahu himself, in a recent encounter with the Northern natives, in which one hundred of his foes were killed, and many eaten, had slain ten victims with his own hand. He had brought to Waikouaiti half a score of the most handsomely tattooed heads, which were preserved and sold to American ships for a keg of gunpowder or two muskets apiece.

The instinct of compassion had scarcely been awakened amongst the Maoris. Hate, cruelty and deceit were universal. Cleanliness and self-control were conspicuous by their absence. Skilful thefts were regarded more as an accomplishment than as a crime. When affliction fell upon a native, the law of muru, or plunder, entitled certain persons to strip the unfortunate person of his canoes and nets and other possessions. It was this custom that had led to the destruction of the Northern Wesleyan Mission Station at Whangaroa in 1827. When Hongi, the Ngapuhi chief, vanquished the natives at Whangaroa and filled the ovens with their bodies, the disaster suffered by the defeated chiefs under whose protection the Wesleyan Mission had been, was, by this law of muru, visited upon the now defenceless missionaries. The mission house was destroyed, the body of the missionary's dead child was dug up for the sake of the blanket in which it was supposed to be wrapped, and the remains were left lying around.

The action of Taiaroa in raiding ' Johnny ' Jones's store at Waikouaiti and appropriating his rum and other commodities is also attributed to the operation of this Maori code of confiscation.

Early in March 1841 a party of Northern canoes arrived in Waikouaiti Bay with a taua, or war party, and but for the action of Mr. Watkin in advancing into the water and making his protest there would have been conflict and bloodshed. As it was, a sham fight took the place of the real one, and this the missionary thought sufficiently horrible.

The opposing groups of natives faced each other on the beach. The bodies of the braves were bedaubed with red earth mixed with shark's oil, whilst the bodies of attendant slaves were blackened with charcoal. They looked a fearsome sight as they danced their haka with every gesture fury could devise. To the accompaniment of filthy invectives, blood-curdling battle-songs and maledictory prayers they lashed themselves to madder desperation. Jerking heads, distorted faces, rolling eyes, protruding tongues and gnashing teeth joined in motion to deride their foes. Slapping their thighs, stamping their bare feet on the sand and emitting volleys of hissing groans in harsh but rhythmic accordance the rivals vented their spleen and wound up by firing their muskets into the swamp as an expression of restored goodwill. They then condescended to fraternize, and after a korero and a feast of peace they parted as friends and gave the missionary a wild ovation.

The receding of the years is a process that is apt to induce a misty memory that limns the horrible realism of the dark days before the Scottish Settlement in the bright tones of chivalry and of romance. In reality those days were gross, reeking, hideous. As we look across the span of crowded years that joins the fiery forties with to-day we can see but little and hear only faint echoes of the swaying conflict as benighted Maoris and free-living white men met the challenge of a militant Methodism to elevate their ethical standards. Watkin and Creed, his successor, had to hew or to blast a way through a bedrock of human badness to the treasure buried beneath. In that task they won success and in the process they incidentally distilled imperishable glory from sordid surroundings.

CHAPTER X

A WHALING STATION IN THE FIERY FORTIES

> Life is not as idle ore,
> But iron dug from central gloom,
> And heated hot with burning fears,
> And dipt in baths of hissing tears
> And batter'd with the shocks of doom
> To shape and use.
>> —TENNYSON : *In Memoriam*, cxviii.

THE Waikouaiti of the fiery forties, it must be remembered, is not the present township and station bearing that name, for the modern borough only received its designation as late as January 1, 1909, by Proclamation in the Government *Gazette*. In the days of the whaler and the pioneer missionary, the name 'Waikouaiti' was attached alike to the river ; to the whalers' village with its ricketty huts stuck about in almost studied disorder on the isthmus near to the river mouth ; and also to the sweeping bay, whose graceful, curving outline stretches northward to the bold promontory known as Matainaka Head, which is drenched for ever with the drifting spray of bursting seas.

The Maori kaika was planted on the bank of the river higher up, and just beneath the shelter of Hau-te-kapakapa, a hill that lay between the isthmus and the pa. The native whares were small and uncleanly, the native women generally dirty and but half-clad in tawdry European clothing. The Wesleyan Mission House occupied the flat, wind-swept top of the hill (adjoining the present Karitane cemetery), a hill that for centuries had been a

WHALERS AND FRENCH WARSHIPS AT PORT OTAGO IN 1840.

noted assembly ground for the native tribes. Perhaps, too, untold ages back, it had given its shadow to uncouth dragons of the slime, in those days before man, or mammal, or bird had yet appeared in the long cycle of the world's onward march, as well as to the gigantic moa birds of later days, whose remains are found in the swamp lying at its foot. But let us picture the scene in 1840 !

Looking landward from the vantage ground of the Mission Hill one can see, across the steaming swamp on which the hot sun is shining, old Hikororoa, a mountain whose shapely shoulders rise to a height of some 2,045 feet. That old monument of Nature is all unconscious that soon he must change his ancient name, that of the apteryx bird that stirred at daylight, for the name of Watkin, the missionary whose coming across the seas spelt the dawning of a brighter morning for the Maori of the South.

On the sandy beach stretching from the base of the hill stands the bay whaling station. To this spot were brought, to be flitched and boiled, the cetacean monsters captured by the ships engaged in bay whaling. The scene of that industry was never an inviting one. Companies of workers, besmeared with grease and blubber, plied their calling around the trying-out pots and the sheerlegs used for lifting the heavy monsters of the deep. From the fires beneath the pots rose dense clouds of smoke, while horrible stenches polluted the atmosphere. Natives greedily clamoured for a share of blubber or whale-flesh, whilst naked children, Maori and half-caste, to give variety to their play, pelted the sea-fowl, that with shrill, discordant shriek, demanded a share of the nauseous spoil, the while more venturesome youngsters harried the snarling kuri and grunting pigs that everywhere gorged themselves with the refuse and the offal. The triers-out often used to peel potatoes by the hundred, string them and then drop them into the boiling oil, where the cooking was soon effected, and the bright yellow potatoes, served with salt, ministered to the gastronomic delight of the company.

G

Erected on the bank of the cliff was a moari, or native swing. This was a tall pole, attached to the top of which were ropes that trailed almost to the ground. The players each grasped a rope, and to the accompaniment of a chant, rhythmically whirled through space, and sometimes relinquished grip, to drop into the water or on to the sand below.

Up till about the year 1830 the Southern Maoris had been living in the Stone Age, and even a decade later there could be seen old men, with infinite patience and skill, grinding rude stone weapons and implements, with which they executed intricate carvings for their whares and their waka or canoes. Until now there had been no real family life amongst the Maoris, but a communism, somewhat modified by the claims of priestcraft and chieftainship. This system served to check enterprise and to discourage effort for individual betterment, as well as to beget indolent and improvident habits. Later evidences of industriousness were the outgrowth of the religion of the Christian missionary.

Upon these primitive people, about the year above mentioned, there swept down a tide of new life, not of the loftiest order, that threatened to engulf them. The native constitution was ill-adapted to counter the clash of alien modes of life and to meet exposure to the physical and moral diseases that had been introduced by lawless white adventurers. When Mr. Watkin came to their aid these simple tribesmen were being overwhelmed in the foreign flood. Upon the pakeha the sense of human unity had scarcely begun to dawn. He conceived a narrow brotherhood, and, colourless himself, did not dream of his fraternity with men of darker hues. Nor did he ever imagine that though for a time the white man might play his own game and profit by the disadvantage of his brown brother, in the end, if life were low and poor for the Maori, it must in consequence be lower and poorer for the pakeha whose breast was yet unstirred by the ideal of a co-operation of the strong holding trusteeship for the weak.

One immediate consequence of the white invasion was the hastening of the process of depopulation then in progress amongst the Maoris. Tribal wars, from which the South had sadly suffered at the hands of the North-erners, the prevalence of infanticide, inherent idleness, filth and superstition had all been causes contributing to decline. The untutored native attributed all sickness to the supernatural, or perhaps the infernal agency of ' taipo.' ' Taipo ' was an imported word that Mr. Watkin found in universal use. He could discover neither its etymology nor its country of origin, but as it appeared to mean ' the devil ' he resolved not to disturb it. Often in his work he prescribed medicine and advised measures for treating the sick, but if the Maoris had the idea that ' taipo ' had seized them, the case for recovery was hopeless. Many a Maori died from no other cause than superstitious fear.

Other influences that operated for the extinction of the Maori in the days of early missionary effort, were the prevalent practice of parents selling young native girls for the use of visiting foreigners ; the circumstance that the males exceeded the females in number ; and the fact that this ill balance of the sexes was aggravated by some of the native women living in concubinage with white whalers. Then deaths in the Maori settlements were much more common than births. The women shirked the responsibility of motherhood. The children were few, and such as there were, were often anæmic and ill-cared for.

From all these causes the instinctive passion for racial immortality was well-nigh extinguished amongst the Maoris. They felt themselves to be a dying race and had sunk into ignoble acquiescence in their own extinction, whilst unprincipled white men, looking on, would not lift a finger to prevent the annihilation of a race whose lands they coveted. These conditions gave Mr. Watkin grave concern. He felt that had his mission begun ten years earlier the process of depopulation might have been arrested, but now only a remnant of these fast-decreasing tribes could hear his gospel, apart from which he saw no hope of their continuance. He discussed the matter earnestly with such chiefs as Korako and Kurakura of Waikouaiti and Noa Paka of Purakanui. These men spoke bitterly of the venereal and other diseases that had been introduced into the country with such tragic results by the crews of visiting ships. They gave affecting accounts of the influenza epidemic brought in 1836 by one of ' Johnny ' Jones's boats, the *Sydney Packet*, and told harrowing tales of the devastation wrought in their kaikas by the visitation of mitari or measles in 1835. Whereas at the dawn of the nineteenth century there were probably some 2,000 natives dwelling at Taiaroa Heads only a few hundred survived in 1840. At Maranuku, better known as Port Molyneux, where there had once been a settlement of 2,000 Maoris, there was but a handful when the missionary made his advent. Places like Purakanui had been reduced from populousness to a mere handful of inhabitants, whilst in other localities, once well peopled, war, disease and vice had left not a single dweller.

Mr. Watkin immediately recognized that the only way to arrest the decline was to bring new interests, the interests of religion, into their lives, in place of the fighting raids and man-eating orgies that once were a paramount concern. His message renewed their interest in living and created a new enthusiasm. With the fresh interest and the extended horizon there was born anew the will to live, and there sprang up the conviction in the Maori mind, that it was, after all, well worth while to bring children into the world.

In any account of Waikouaiti in the year 1840 mention must be made of the agricultural settlement that Mr. ' Johnny ' Jones was establishing at Matainaka. Bay whaling was now a dwindling industry, and foreseeing the day when it would no longer be remunerative, Jones had sent down from Sydney, as early as 1838, some fifteen head of cattle, which meanwhile would enable beef to be bred on the spot instead of bringing salt meat in his ships. He then, as recorded in another chapter, set about acquiring extensive areas of land from the Maoris, securing, so it is said, one large estate for a bag of black sugar, and other rolling domains for modest quantities of rum and tobacco.

A few weeks before the arrival of Mr. Watkin the *Magnet* had brought a number of pakeha passengers for the agricultural settlement of the shipowner, and as these constituted the first regular shipload of settlers for Otago, and as many of their descendants still maintain honourable citizenship in the Province, it is well to put their names on record.   The following list is based upon those published by Dr. T. M. Hocken and Dr. Robert McNab, but I have corrected some obvious errors in transcription in the list of the latter gentleman, and supplied from Mr. Watkin's early mission records now in my possession, the Christian names of the wives of a number of these pathfinders.

The honour roll of these settlers in the days before ' The ' Settlement of 1848, is as follows :

John and Margaret Beale and their daughter.
David and Hannah Carey and their daughter.
Benjamin and Elizabeth Coleman and two daughters.
William Coleman and his wife.
George and Harriet Glover, and a son and a daughter.
Thomas Hawkins and his wife.
Thomas Jones, his wife, son and daughter.
William and Maria Kennard, two daughters and a son.
Thomas and Elizabeth Pasco, and a son.
Frederick and Harriet Prior.
John Pullar, his wife and son.
William Stirling and his wife.
William Trotter.

Evidently George Glover remarried for after the year 1842 the name of his wife appears in the records as ' Grace.'

Dr. McNab, whose list was evidently compiled from an old Sydney passenger list, gives the following names not included in Dr. Hocken's summary :—C. Flower and J. Street with their families, and W. George, J. Reid and W. Johnstone ; but such records as I have do not show if these people actually sailed from the New South Wales port.

But perhaps the most notable feature of the Waikouaiti whaling station was the Mission House and its occupants on Hau-te-kapakapa Hill. When James Watkin and Hannah, his wife, landed at Waikouaiti at noon on Saturday, May 16, 1840, with their five little children, bearing the names James Entwistle, William Jackson, Jabez Bunting, Hannah Jane and Edwin Iredale, they were asked by Mr. J. Jones, who had given a pledge of a comfortable Mission House, to share some miserable lodgings in quarters occupied by Thomas Jones, the brother of the station-owner. Here they made themselves as comfortable as possible over the Sunday, and on Monday, having initiated his evangelizing enterprise, Mr. Watkin, with his family, crossed to the agricultural settlement with Mr. Jones, who told him that his house had been built there.

Mr. Watkin found the place provided was totally inadequate for his family needs, and recognized immediately that living at Matainaka would defeat the main object of his presence in New Zealand, namely the spiritual welfare of the aboriginal inhabitants. He straightway resolved upon securing a temporary residence of some kind at Waikouaiti itself. Two days later he selected the site already referred to at Hau-te-kapakapa Hill. On this stood a native whare in an unfinished state. This was acquired and carpenters were set to work to weatherboard the sides so as to render it habitable. When completed it was miserable enough but the best then available. On May 26, the parents with their five children took possession of the hut, being composed of one room divided by a curtain, which was not too large for two people, and resolved to be content until they could enlarge their borders. A few glimpses of the missionary family will not be profitless, especially as they touch intimately the life of their domestic circle.

The process of unpacking certain indispensable articles of furniture and of getting the house in order drew a crowd of natives, whose presence proved somewhat of a hindrance. By the month of August a new house was in course of erection. This contained four small rooms and an attic. It was built of planks and had a shingle roof and boasted the first brick chimney built in the South Island. This was constructed of Sydney fire-bricks, one of which lies before me as I write. This new house, though an improvement upon the old, was so small that the presence of one extra native, when the family was collected, was a serious inconvenience, more especially as experience had shown that, for sufficient reasons, ' proximity was to be avoided by all who could accomplish it.' When the whare that had formerly done duty as a home was vacated, it was used as a school and preaching house, and in it, Mr. Watkin records, he ' sought to teach the Maoris the truths of the Christian religion, which alone could banish the super-stitions that enslaved their minds, and restrain them from the bloodshed in which they delighted.' No trace of whare or mission house now remains save the foundation of the chimney stack, for the building was, many years ago, removed to Seacliff to be used as a store and ultimately fell before the devouring flame.

The comfortless Mission House, which had an earthern floor, was both damp and cold. The Watkin's had not known a real winter for ten long years, and the children, all but one born in the tropics, and he in Sydney, felt the cold of these southern latitudes acutely. Early in June 1840 some improvement was effected by flooring the place with planks. The winter of that year proved a bitter one.

Rain deluged the low-lying lands and swelled the volume
of the river as it rumbled to the sea. Frost gripped the
and with its unseen hand, fledged the flax with icy feathers
rills made the reeds look like ' polished lances in a hostile
field.' The tempest of fleecy flakes adorned the hills
with its ghostly drapery. Trees wailed at the whipping
of the winter wind. Within the Mission House, when the
natives had been dismissed from evening school, the
family beguiled the long winter evenings with *Chambers'*
Encyclopædia and other books, that stored the minds of the
children of that humble Methodist manse with rich resources
of knowledge and of wisdom.

A few incidents may fittingly conclude this chapter,
which, though not belonging strictly to the year 1840,
reflect the conditions that were shared in common by the
pioneers of that period. To the Waikouaiti Settlement
in the winter of 1841 the sharp and meagre face of Famine
was disclosed in menacing mood. For five months no
boat had arrived from Sydney and no contact was established with civilized life. The natives had to go far afield
in search of food. Their main diet was aruhe or fern root,
which was beaten with a patu, and though disagreeable
to the taste of the uninitiated, and being rough eating,
owing to the presence in it of woody particles, possessed
a certain amount of nutriment. The whaling and agricultural stations were, records Mr. Watkin, almost destitute
of food. For months the settlers from Sydney subsisted
on pipis and Maori cabbage, and one tells of having eaten
blancmange made of starch. For weeks the missionary
family was reduced to a diet of potatoes and salt, with
damper on Sundays. On August 23, Mr. Watkin wrote
in his diary that they were on the point of want and had
never before been so poorly circumstanced. A week later
the distressed community was gladdened by the sound of
a gun fired from the *Magnet*, which had that evening
arrived from Sydney with supplies.

One day during the summer of 1843 Mr. Watkin with

THE ANCHORAGE AT OTAGO HEADS IN 1840

his wife and several of the younger children went up the Waikouaiti River for a family picnic. They tied their boat at the river-bank and were seated for lunch when a naki, or wild cat, came along with a captured bird in its mouth. A Maori youth gave chase and the naki dropped the bird, which the native at once gave to Edwin Iredale Watkin, a laddie of some four summers. The child went to the riverside to put the bird in the boat, and in doing so accidentally slipped into the river. His long absence aroused comment, and Jabez, a brother two years older, was sent after him. The elder boy saw the bird in the boat, and then, turning, caught sight of Edwin lying in several feet of water with a number of tuna, or eels, surrounding him. He gave a hurried alarm and soon the unfortunate little fellow was brought ashore, and restorative measures, that happily proved successful, were applied. Thus was saved to the Church and the world the richly fruitful life of the Rev. Dr. Watkin, who himself told me of his accident. Fuller particulars of this were afterwards related to me by the brother responsible for his rescue, while I was a guest within his hospitable home at Nukualofa, in the Friendly Islands, within which group, in the home of Taufa-ahau, who later became King George I of Tonga, he was born on March 31, 1837, and where for many years he was President of the Free Wesleyan Church of Tonga.

The circumstance that the home of the missionary, representing a new method of life and a new standard of conduct, was not the least contribution of Mr. Watkin to New Zealand's life, invests these details with some measure of interest, and excuses the inclusion of domestic matters within this narrative. Such a matter was the departure of the two eldest boys of the missionary, on January 3, 1842, for Sydney, in their educational interest, as Waikouaiti then offered few advantages in that regard. Sickness, too, invaded the home. Mrs. Watkin, delicately nurtured as she had been amidst the refinements of a cultured English home, had her cross to bear. She suffered

serious illness and endured almost chronic martyrdom
from that distressing affliction, tic doloreaux. In the
cramped mission house she twice went down to the gates
of death to bring back two new lives, those of her New
Zealand babes, Joseph Hebblewhite and John Wesley
Watkin. Mr. Watkin, too, was constantly in ill-health,
and those who read the records of his experiences will not
marvel at that fact. The beginning of 1843 saw him broken
in health, weak in body and depressed in spirits. Days
and nights of pain were his portion and he often felt he
was looking death in the face. He flogged himself to a
faithful discharge of public duties that he could only
accomplish with difficulty. At about this period there
arrived in Otago harbour the Bremen whaleship *Juliana*,
carrying a surgeon, who on being consulted administered
powerful medicines and prescribed ' cupping.' Nine
glasses were used. The scarifier contained fifteen lancets,
and two applications were made to each place. The
patient was a good deal weakened by this heroic treatment,
but even then chronicled his fear that an insufficient
quantity of blood had been taken to ensure relief !

Despite all disabilities Mr. Watkin soon began to win
out. The natives began to rise from sunken savagery.
Community houses, in which all sat or slept together,
fell into disuse. Each family managed to build its own
whare, and family habits and household customs showed
signs of being revolutionized. Cleanliness was taught,
habits of industry were inculcated, growing girls were
instructed in domestic arts and the use of the needle.
The Christian habits of life were imitated, and amid the
wreckage of an ancient order a new began to emerge.
Signs of success became manifest. They were like an index
to a book, or like an alphabet to a language or a literature.
The index is imperfect. The alphabet is fragmentary.
But both are like the outer court of a great temple,
suggesting something bigger, better, and nobler. The
outlines of the temple that James Watkin built will disclose

themselves as we follow the fortunes of his work and trace
out the operation of the influences that he set working
in the life of Southern New Zealand in days of long
ago.

Chapter XI

THE LABYRINTH OF THE LANGUAGE

What if this work's great hardness was concealed
From us, until so far upon our way
That no escape remained for us, no retreat—
Lest, being at an earlier hour revealed,
We might have shrunk too weakly from the heat,
And shunned the burden of this fiery day.
                              —ARCHBISHOP TRENCH.

WHEN James Watkin was commissioned to inaugurate his mission at Waikouaiti he fully recognized that the initial step in the evangelization of the Maori was to gain mastery of his speech, the vocabulary of which was singularly opulent for a race that stood on the barbaric culture plane.

During his long voyage from Sydney in the brig *Regia*, Mr. Watkin, who was an expert in the Tongan tongue, spent considerable time in the study of Maori, using as text-books the publications of the Wesleyan Mission Press at Mangungu, and of the Church of England Press at Paihia. Upon his arrival at Waikouaiti, however, he speedily found that the Northern and Southern dialects differed so greatly that the available publications would be practically valueless in his work. Within a fortnight of his coming he records that he had read to the natives from the New Testament published in the North, and he adds the comment :—' It appears a strange language to this people. Many of the words bear a resemblance to the words spoken here, whilst others are quite distinct.'

Mr. Watkin was not solitary in his experience of the

difficulties arising from the marked divergence of dialect. A few weeks after he came to Waikouaiti, Major Bunbury paid his historic visit to Otago in Her Majesty's ship *Herald*, to secure the attachment of the signatures of the Southern chiefs to the famous Treaty of Waitangi. This gallant officer was accompanied by Mr. Edward Marsh Williams, son of the Rev. Henry Williams, a practised interpreter, whose duty it was to explain the nature of the document to the chiefs. Dr. Robert McNab, in his book, *The Old Whaling Days* records that so great was the difficulty this gifted linguist experienced in making himself understood, that he had to seek the services of a visiting native, who was familiar with the Ngapuhi dialect, to act as his intermediary.

Another distinguished visitor who met with similar difficulty was Bishop Selwyn, who made his first acquaintance with Otago in January 1844, and was for two days a guest of the Wesleyan missionary at Waikouaiti. Mr. Watkin, with gracious and characteristic courtesy, paid the Bishop the compliment of asking him to address and to catechize the natives of the Wesleyan Mission. Subsequently when writing in very cordial terms to his friend and colleague, the Rev. Samuel Ironside, about the visit of His Lordship, Mr. Watkin said,

' We don't understand his Maori much this way.'

The linguistic dilemma in which such proficient Maori scholars as Bishop Selwyn and Mr. E. M. Williams were placed by the dissimilarity of the Southern and Northern speech is a strange commentary upon the record of Bishop Pompallier, of the Roman Catholic Mission, who paid a flying visit to Otakou Heads in November 1840. This prelate's party included as an intermediary for speech to the natives, one Father Comte, whom Bishop Pompallier says he brought from Hokianga, where, he adds, ' he had learnt the Maori language passably.'

With this passable knowledge of a Northern dialect, the party claimed to have evangelized the natives at

Otakou Heads at the end of ten days. The Bishop, however, chronicled his chagrin that for lack of money and of men he must in the future leave this field to the Protestants. But of this more anon.

Referring to his own initial philological perplexities, Mr. Watkin, within a fortnight of his arrival, wrote in his Journal that it would be necessary to begin afresh to form an alphabet, and to reduce to writing ' this hitherto unwritten language.' He had also to compile a vocabulary and construct a grammar. His only dictionary was that to be read on the lips of the natives themselves. Anxious as he was to instruct the minds of the natives, he could not begin to lay a literary foundation until he had mastered the various linguistic processes and attained a grammatical as well as a colloquial knowledge of the language. It was not easy work to act the pioneer in this respect. The verbal complexities of the language constituted a formidable labyrinth, and Mr. Watkin said that he felt like a man travelling in the dark along unfamiliar paths. Still he spent no regrets upon the necessity confronting him, rejoicing that he could thus do something to prepare the path for others. He resolutely set himself to learn the vernacular sounds by imitation, and to acquire and teach the art of precise articulation. To do this he had to master the vital distinction between breath and voice, to consider sounds, both vowel and consonantal, from the viewpoint of analysis, to note the operation of the law of poise which governs the alternations of light and heavy syllables in the music of speech, and having done this to reduce to writing the miracle of language in all its complex unity.

Watkin found that the natural instability of the Maori character reflected itself in the instability of the Maori language. Like many semi-civilized communities the Maoris regarded sound-changes more lightly than the higher peoples do. They showed a tendency to the exercise of phonetic license. They were often careless and incorrect in the pronunciation of consonants, while changes and transpositions crept into their speech almost unnoticed. Even amongst Northern tribes familiar words often revealed rather remarkable interchanges of letters. That peculiarity was accentuated in the South, where the variations often made for a certain harshness of speech. Other elements of irregularity and irrationality, both orthographical and etymological, were met with, whilst grammatical forms and grammatical functions at times corresponded but very imperfectly. Mr. Watkin found that the Southern Maoris made frequent use of the letter ' l,' which had no place in the Northern alphabet. The ' ng ' of the North usually appeared as ' k ' in the South. For example, ' kainga ' became ' kaika,' ' tohunga ' appeared as ' tohuka,' whilst ' Tangaroa,' the notable god of the sea, was known to the Southerners as ' Takaloa.' The ' wh ' of the North, which has a soft breathing sound similar to the ' ph ' in our word ' cenotaph,' was, amongst the Southern natives, usually sharpened into ' f,' a letter unknown in the Northern alphabet. Concerning this last peculiarity so capable a scholar as the Rev. W. Stack thought that such words as ' fenua ' (the ground), ' fakana ' (judgement), ' fakapai ' (to bless), and ' fakatika ' (to make straight), and scores of similar words, the use of which was noted by Mr. Watkin, were simply examples of depraved Maori, for the introduction of which the whalers were responsible. That opinion, I understand, is not now held by the best authorities. All these variations, rendering as they did, the Northern publications of little value in the South, greatly increased the difficulties of the pioneer missionary. The adoption of the soft and euphonious dialect of the Waikato Maoris by the Anglican and Wesleyan missionaries for the translation of the Scriptures, gradually resulted in dialectical differences being modified or obliterated by that all-pervading literary standard for the language.

The Rev. James Watkin's task was not only that of

evangelizing the heathen. He had to convert their language, enrich and baptize their vocabulary and make it a fit vehicle to express Divine truth. To write idiomatically is to employ words in a fashion hallowed by long usage. That presented not the least of his perplexities. Differences in idiom make it impossible always to give a literal translation. While possessing a vocabulary capable of copious and fairly exact word-connotation, the Maoris had no words to express some of the vital facts of revelation, nor had they any concept of some of the virtues of Christian character. They had no word for conscience or for hope. Their proverb, ' Aroha mai, aroha atu ' (Love received demands love returned) suggests grateful feeling, but they had such little idea of the grace of gratitude that Mr. Watkin, in order to fill a gap in Maori speech, borrowed from Tonga the word ' fakafetai ' to signify ' thanks,' and then had to create the emotion expressed by the word grafted upon their language. Thus did he make words the windows of eternal things.

The missionary path-finder picked up Maori words and phrases with remarkable facility. Within three weeks of his advent he recorded that he could manage to understand and make himself understood on most common subjects. Everywhere he went he carried a pocket-book bound in red morocco, and noted down every word he heard, supplying the meaning whenever and wherever possible. Soon he had accumulated a collection of some two thousand words and phrases. This vocabulary is still preserved in the Hocken Library in Dunedin, and when it is read in the light of his diary one can often determine when and where he gleaned his verbal harvest. For much of his progress he was indebted to his native servant, ' Tommy Roundhead ' whom he subjected to constant catechizing. Words were captured and catalogued, colloquial phrases written and remembered, and sentences were contrived until fluent intercourse was established with the natives. So rapid was the progress of Mr. Watkin

WESLEYAN MISSION HOUSE AT WAIKOUAITI, 1840.

Showing the First Brick Chimney in the South Island of New Zealand.

in overcoming linguistic difficulties and in mastering
the complex grammatical structure of the language that
exactly seventeen weeks after his arrival, namely on
September 13, 1840, he preached to the natives extem-
poraneously in their mother tongue. His modesty over
this achievement manifests itself in the entry in his Journal,
which runs :

> ' I have often felt something like shame that I have been
> so long as four months in acquiring an ability to deliver
> myself extempore, but the difficulties of acquiring a language
> which has never been previously learnt by any, can only be
> appreciated by those who have had a similar task. Now
> my way will be comparatively easy. I have had many
> hindrances, and still have, but hope to master every diffi-
> culty and lay a foundation upon which others may build.'

In addition to all his pastoral work among both races,
and the tasks incidental to inaugurating a new mission,
Mr. Watkin had, within less than six months of his arrival,
done a considerable amount of literary and educational
spade-work. Schools had been established at Waikouaiti
and Matainaka and some natives had been taught to read
a little. He had compiled a fairly extensive vocabulary,
written some short prayers which the natives had learnt,
composed a few hymns for congregational singing, translated part of the Liturgy, rendered a portion of the Wesleyan
Methodist Catechism, No. 1, into the Southern dialect,
and dispatched an elementary Maori reading book, which
embodied the alphabet, some simple sentences, the Ten
Commandments and other matter in the Ngaitahu dialect
to the Wesleyan Mission Press at Mangungu for publication.
This volume, which was the first book in the Southern
dialect ever issued from the printing press, suffered long
delay in publication, and for over a year after its preparation
the missionary impatiently awaited its coming.

For some reason, however, the book was not printed
at Mangungu, but by T. Frood, of King Street, East

H

Sydney. No copy is known to have survived, but the Rev. W. J. Watkin, a son of the pioneer, records that some of the sentences were :

Hi te ika	Catch the fish
Homai tou rika	Lend us your hand
Haere ki waho	Go outside
Kowai te pakeha.	Who is the stranger

Concerning the hymns he had translated or composed, Mr. Watkin acknowledged that some were of imperfect scansion, and he disclaimed the possession of the poetic gift. He, however, contrived to avoid such blunders as were perpetrated by one heaven-sent translator, who, when rendering the familiar hymn, ' Showers of Blessing,' into the vernacular, set the native congregation singing :—

Let some squirts now squirt on me, even me.

Nor did he fall into the mistake of the interpreter unfamiliar with English colloquialisms, and who failed to catch the undertones of idiom and meaning in the phrase describing how a man was ' tickled to death,' and rendered it—' he was scratched until he died.'

The creditable record outlined above had been established early in November 1840, and prior to the date, when Bishop Pompallier said of Mr. Watkin, ' He is studying the language of the natives in order to instruct them hereafter.'

By August 1840, the Wesleyan Missionary had his native school in full swing. The class for men and boys assembled in his kitchen at early morn and that for women and girls in the evening. In the school work he was assisted by his devoted wife and their two elder boys, James and William, who were aged respectively, nine and seven years. Chiefs and people, old and young, were all eager to learn, and having learned, were anxious to communicate their scant stock of knowledge to others. Mr.

Watkin describes the scene in the crowded room at the
Mission House. Grizzled old warriors with faces furrowed
by time as well as by the tattooing instrument, and hot-
blooded Maori youths, all ambitious to learn, are conning
the pages of little books containing the alphabet and simple
reading lessons penned by the hand of the missionary
himself ; and whilst he is teaching some, others of the
dusky company are soliciting the help of his little lads,
with such questions as

' E ha tenei, Hemi ? ' (What is this, James ?) or ' E ha
tena, Wiriamu ? ' (What is that, William ?).

The sight of these Maoris, who knew how to carve the
stems and sterns of their canoes and how to trace upon
the face the marks that distinguish the warrior, learning
to write on slates and paper the words they had received
by tradition from their fathers was a sight that might
equally stir the soul of the artist or give pleasure to a
philosopher.

The absence of printed books greatly distressed and
hampered the missionary, and until the reading primer
which he had prepared over fifteen months previously
came to hand on December 13, 1841, Mr. Watkin had the
dreary task of writing by hand all the school books he
needed. At first he wrote the vowels and consonants on
pieces of cardboard. These symbols he sought to impress
on the speculum of the scholars, and from the alphabet
he advanced to syllables, words, sentences and paragraphs.
But even his prolific pen could not keep pace with the
demands of his voracious native pupils. As his scholars
progressed in knowledge he also wrote copies of almanacs
and prayer-books, as well as puka whakauro, or books of
reference, for the native helpers whom he had won from
heathenism and trained for service. Often he was driven
to desperation by the shortage of equipment for his school-
work. Copy books, slates, pens and ink were frequently
in short supply. On one occasion not a spare slate was
available to meet the desire of a native who offered the

missionary half-a-crown for this coveted aid to learning. On another occasion writing upon slates was altogether suspended for lack of slate pencils.

The spread of the arts of reading and writing among the Maoris brought its embarrassments. In June of 1842 one of the natives, who had acquired the useful accomplishment and acted as amanuensis to that notable chief, Tuhawaiki, wrote requesting from the missionary the gift of a bottle of brandy. Mr. Watkin replied that he did not possess such a thing, and, moreover, would not have given it if he had.

On another occasion five or six letters arrived together, all fairly written, and most asking for writing materials. One requested not only ' rauhamoa ' (paper) but sealing wax and wafers as well! Specimens of early Maori attempts at penmanship are preserved in the Mission Marriage Register. On June 19, 1843, four Maori couples who had been previously united conformably to native custom, were married according to the rites of the Christian Church. Three bridegrooms, a bride and four Maori witnesses all attached their signatures. Commenting upon this Mr. Watkin wrote that he expected the register would be a curiosity to a professor in caligraphy. Yes! it would. But it stands also as a tribute to his own work as a teacher of penmanship and a creator of a new type of native manhood.

It might fairly be claimed for Mr. Watkin that he was the pioneer in organizing a system of education in the South Island of New Zealand. He established and conducted schools at Waikouaiti and Matainaka with the aid of his wife and two boys. Later at Moeraki to the north, and as far south as Stewart Island, he sent partially instructed natives to preach and to teach. When in March 1844 he visited Jacob's River, where the civil authorities were just commencing a school for Anglo-Maori children, he visited the school and gave valuable assistance to the master.

The educational foundations laid first by Watkin and Creed, and the subsequent efforts of the civil government, which were fostered by these missionaries, prepared the way for the commencement of the educational activities of the Scottish settlers, who, on September 24, 1848, began their efforts in this direction by opening their first school in Dunedin.

All the educational work of the Wesleyan Mission, as well as its spiritual ministrations, was absolutely free, alike to pakeha and to Maori, although it was carried on at considerable cost to the Missionary Society, which spent large sums upon the South Island enterprise, until its activities, in common with most Christian work throughout New Zealand, suffered partial but tragic eclipse through the consequences of the lamentable Maori War.

Chapter XII

WINNING AN UPWARD WAY

Let no man think that sudden, in a minute,
All is accomplished and the work is done ;—
Though with thine earliest dawn thou shouldst begin it
Scarce were it ended in thy setting sun.

Oh the regret, the struggle and the failing !
Oh the days desolate and useless years !
Vows in the night, so fierce and unavailing !
Stings of my shame and passion of my tears !

F. W. H. MYERS.

SOUTHERN New Zealand in 1840 was not merely a place,
it was a condition. It was not only a geographical unit,
but also a psychological one. The aboriginal inhabitants
were terrified with superstition. White men from over
the sea had lapsed, many of them, into virtual paganism.
When the ancestors of these Maoris had come to the
coasts of Ao-tea-roa they were splendid specimens of
physical humanity, strong in body, alert in mind, original
in thought, keen in insight, poetic in speech and with a
spirit of heroic mould. Yet so unequal in grain were
they that at times they were fiends incarnate. Watkin
found the Otago Maoris crushed between a cruel heathenism
and a degraded civilization. He set himself to ameliorate
their unhappy lot and to work for their redemption. He
ate their bread when it was eatable, but oftener shared his
own. He slept in their crowded whares and received them
into his home. He shared in their sorrows oblivious to
his own, and dispensed medicine to men in whose minds

sickness and sorcery were one and indivisible. Thus by the wondrous alchemy of self-forgetting love he transmuted his own disabilities into the gold of great achievement and carried his brown-skinned brothers over the abyss of superstition to the solid ground of rational religious faith.

On the morning of his first Sunday in Southern Maoriland James Watkin was astir sufficiently early to see the vanishing stars closing their gates as the sun peeped over the edge of a rose-rimmed sea. The cloak of dusk was slipping from the heaving shoulders of the breathing hills. The birds of dawnlight were crying to the new day from distant tree-tops. The facets of the rustling leaves were twinkling at the quivering pressure of gentle breezes that spilt cupfuls of fragrance as they rose from their hiding places and stole on soft tip-toe across the drowsy, narrow world that would claim the missionary for four fateful years to come. The brightness of the morning brushed the gloomy reveries of the dark from the deeps of Watkin's soul and left the perfume of high purpose upon his spirit as he took up his task.

When the hour for his first service arrived the eye of the preacher ranged over a strange congregation. A number of men from the whaling gang were present, also a company of the agricultural settlers and a considerable number of Maoris who, whilst unable to understand the preacher, were curious to observe the ' karakia bora,' or English mode of worship. Some of the natives wore only a blanket, others simply a flax-leaf mat tied around the neck and hanging over the shoulders to the knees. Others were unclad save for a maro worn around the loins or a kokomo or long skirt girdled with a tatua. A few looked rather ludicrous wearing indiscriminately some portion of European raiment that revealed rather than concealed their persons. Others had well rubbed their tattooed bodies with oil from the weka or wood hen. Their faces were bedaubed with yellow ochre, an occasional feather adorned their hair, while boars' tusks, inserted in pierced ear lobes, were not uncommon. A little cluster of Maori children in Nature's nudity looked on with eyes full of wonder.

Weighted with a sense of profound responsibility Mr. Watkin announced the theme of the first Christian sermon preached in Southern New Zealand. He took as his text the words, ' This is a faithful saying and worthy of all acceptation that Christ Jesus came into the world to save sinners ' (1 Timothy i. verse 15). He at once caught the attention and the gaze of his hearers. From eye to eye a signal ran. That signal was, on the part of brown men and white, a deep, real, inarticulate cry for God, and on the preacher's part a positive confidence in the power of the gospel of Jesus Christ to meet their every need.

The whares in which the natives lived were, for the most part, squat shanties made of logs and fern trunks. These were entered by crawling on all fours through ' doorways ' some two feet square. Above these apertures was usually another of similar size to afford light and ventilation. Into these filthy and vile-smelling whares, with their earthen floors, the people crowded. Under such conditions it is obvious that what we know as the sanctities of home could scarcely exist.

The well-being of any people depends upon the family unit just as the health of the body depends upon the structural cells of which it is made up. If the home centre is degraded the race can hope for no true, noble or vigorous life. In the home of the missionary the Maoris now saw exhibited a new type of family life marked by refinement, self-sacrifice and service. From various motives they would crowd into the mission house, the air of which speedily became thick with the acid odour of sweat-soiled skins that often bore the unwashed grime of many days.

The loveliness and the charm of domestic life are

Signature	Name
Haimona Pita Mutu	SIMON PETER MUTU.
Hoani Weteri Korako	JOHN WESLEY KORAKO.
Hohaia Otane Pokaitara	JOSIAH OTANE POKAITARA.
Tiare Weteri te kaahu	CHARLES WESLEY te Kaahu
Mohi Puhorokai	MOSES PUHOROKAI.
Horomona Pohio	SOLOMON POHIO
Noa Paka	NOAH PARKER.
Rawiri te maire	DAVID te Maire.
Hemi Wakena Mahaka	JAMES WATKIN MAHAKA.

SIGNATURES OF CHIEFS AND TEACHERS, 1841.
WESLEYAN MARRIAGE REGISTER.

dependent upon the fulfilment by women of their vocation as home builders, and that vocation had never been sensed by the native female. Very few had any true idea of cleanliness. The old-time Maori wife regarded it as a compliment to her husband not to wash during the frequent and protracted absence of her ' man ' from home. The faces of women and girls were often smeared with the red juice of a wild berry. Their hair was ill-kempt. Some incessantly smoked tobacco, and even the crying babe was ' soothed,' or drugged, by a suck at the short, black pipe which was usually held between lips black with tobacco juice, or, when it was not in use, stuck through a hole in the lobe of the ear. Their moral force had been sapped by subtle seductions and some had fallen easy victims to the passions of the pakeha.

The Maori in the earlier half of the nineteenth century had few necessities and no luxuries. A being without a future he lived in the passing hour amidst alternations of unwelcome fasts and gluttonous revels. Fighting, fishing and pig-hunting were his chief pursuits. A lover of ease he positively hated anything like avoidable work. When urged to industrious efforts his invariable reply was ' By and by.' He worked only as much as was necessary to sustain existence, and the occupations that engage the higher races of men found little part in his life. Mr. Watkin says that after planting their potatoes they would neglect them for months at a stretch, while only the pressure of necessity could drive them to dig and prepare the fern root that annually saved them from famine.

The missionary found the natives disinclined to render any service without pay and for this their demands were exorbitant. If they bestowed a gift, by the law of paremata they looked for a greater in return. The grace of gratitude was absent. They were content to receive every boon he could bestow yet forgot their gratitude in the enjoyment of favours left unacknowledged. After months of heart-breaking toil he wrote :—' I have not a single instance of gratitude to record, but many of the contrary sort, were I so disposed.' He later made the discovery that his labours had not been all resultless, and as he looked at these brown-skinned people, with natures changed by his gospel he said, ' Natives like these I know I shall not find in New Zealand.'

Waikouaiti in 1840 was one of the most isolated stations in the mission field. During the whole of Mr. Watkin's term there the Wesleyan Mission brigantine *Triton* did not call at his station nor was he once visited by the General Superintendent, the Rev. John Waterhouse, in his periodical tours of the missionary stations in the South Seas. Until the Rev. Samuel Ironside came to Cloudy Bay in December 1840, the nearest brother ministers of Watkin were those of the Wesleyan Mission Stations in the North Island, and communication with them was by way of Sydney—a circuitous route of some 3,000 miles. Until he met two of his brethren at the District Meeting in Wellington on October 21, 1843, he had not seen the face of a brother missionary for three years and five months, and during that long period he was imprisoned by narrow tasks and a hum-drum routine that was dull and deadening. He had no comradeship with intellectual equals nor any real spiritual fellowship. Often his loftiest thoughts had to be caged in his own lonely heart.

The monotony of his life was, however, broken by rare and fleeting friendly visitors. These included the captains of two American ships that were at Otago harbour when the *Herald* paid her visit in 1840 to secure the signatures of the Southern chiefs to the Treaty of Waitangi, and who, on June 14, both attended the services at Waikouaiti and Matainaka ; the chaplain of the Bremen whaleship *Juliana*, who called on him on February 4, 1843, and Captain Barker, of the whaleship *Lancaster*, who paid a visit on New Year Day, 1844, and who left with Mr. Watkin some combs that were distributed amongst the Maori girls, much to their delight.

The difficulty of communication added an intensity of loneliness to the lot of the missionary that it is hard to imagine. Sometimes native messengers travelling overland carried missives between Waikouaiti and Cloudy Bay, but these messengers were unreliable. Any small difficulty or vagrant impulse or the enticements of a good square meal would deter them from their purpose or switch them aside for indefinite periods.

Mails from England were infrequent. Periodicals often arrived eighteen months and two years after publication. When the Wesleyan Conference of 1843 was meeting in London Mr. Watkin had not received the Minutes of the Conferences of the two previous years. On March 29, 1841, he received from England a letter of some importance. It had been mailed two years and one month previously, and besides giving an account of his father's death it contained the provisions of his father's will, which gave him certain benefits contingent upon his presence in England within a specified time. That limit had been exceeded by one month when the letter came to hand! Mr. Watkin had not anticipated a loss he was so ill able to bear, but with the resignation of a Stoic he wrote in his Journal, ' Where the delay has arisen I cannot tell, nor is it necessary now to inquire.'

The missionary was often hampered by shortage of equipment for his work. Sickness invaded his home. His own health was broken by toil and misunderstanding. He saw his work falling short of full success because his unflinching fidelity in denouncing human evil brought from some of his fellow-countrymen hatred and opposition. Yet with a love that was pain-drenched he climbed to conquest.

The earliest evidence of the influence of Mr. Watkin began to be manifest within three brief weeks of his arrival at Waikouaiti. With clear vision he saw that the spiritual values that are created by the Sabbath Day could not be looked for in a community where Sunday was secularised.

The desecration of the Lord's Day by Europeans had created an environment of irreligion that was a real menace to the moral health of the region.

Although he had then been able only imperfectly to set before the Maoris the claims of the Sabbath, he records on June 6, 1840, that they had begun already to abstain from Sunday labour. A fortnight later he states that a native chief had decided to cancel a projected Sunday trip to Moeraki. Three years later he recorded with satisfaction that not one native at Waikouaiti or Moeraki, and only two at Otakou, would now join the whaling parties, their principal objection being that it led to a desecration of the Lord's Day.

Although Mr. Watkin had officiated at an Anglo-Maori wedding as early as January 27, 1841, the first purely Maori marriages took place on June 19 of that year, when four native couples who had previously been married according to their own customs observed the Christian ordinance. The contracting parties deserve to have their names put on record.

They were :

> Haimona Pita Mutu to Pi.
> Rawiri Te Maire to Heikuna.
> Tiare Weteri Te Kahu to Riria Weteri Wharekauri.
> Heremia Tahara Whana to Roko Tahana.

The witnesses were Hoani Weteri Korako, Hohaia Otane Pokaitara, Mohi Puhorokai and Horomona Pohio.

By 1842 the sounds calling to Christian worship could be heard in many Maori villages in Southern New Zealand. In some places, as at Moeraki, the ' bell ' was a kohua or round iron pot. In others old musket barrels suspended by cords were used to summon to the services. Waikouaiti itself rejoiced in the possession of a sweet-toned bell that had originally done duty on an early Botany Bay convict-ship. Later it had been acquired by John Jones and had been used as ship's bell on the *Magnet*, then trading to New Zealand. By Jones it was handed over to Mr. Watkin for the Wesleyan Mission at Waikouaiti. Subsequently Jones removed it and it was placed at the Presbyterian Church Reserve in Dunedin, which thus became known as Bell Hill. Here it did duty until 1851, when it was superseded by a bell that now lies cracked beneath the shadow of First Church. The old mission bell itself now rests in the Early Settlers' Museum in Dunedin.

Mr. Watkin has put on record that the singing at the Maori services was not unpleasing. There is no mention of any instrumental accompaniments, although during 1840 Mr. Watkin wrote that the Maori word for a harmonium was ' herekana.'

It is worth recording that the first public celebration of the Holy Communion and the first administration of this Sacrament to Maori participants in the Southern parts of New Zealand took place on January 29, 1843, when Mr. and Mrs. Watkin and seven native men partook of the sacred symbols that made visible and vivid the fact that for their sake a Saviour's body had been broken like the loaf and His blood had run like the flowing wine. In other lands that sobering spectacle had for centuries borne its testimony to a love that never grows old. It had outlasted the vicissitudes of nations and empires, and now to these simple tribesmen its silent eloquence witnessed to their heritage of a new life. It brought home to them the realization of their vital fellowship with God and of the reality of the bond that united them to the pakeha missionary and his wife whose lives had been so completely given up for them. The names of the native communicants were :—Iraia Tukiwaha, Haimona Pita Mutu, Paura Tua, Aperahama Karu, Mohi Puhorokai, Rawiri Te Maire, and Toati Witiwhiri Papakawha. All but the last-mentioned bore Scriptural names, and he had received the name of Whitefield in its Maori form.

It was a constant joy to the heart of the pioneer preacher

to see his congregations gathering for worship at Waikouaiti and elsewhere with their New Testaments and hymn books carried in bags or in baskets slung about the neck, and holding the place formerly occupied by the powder flask and the cartridge box. Firearms had hitherto been the most acceptable medium of exchange in trade but now the natives would readily barter their muskets for Testaments and for the tools of industry.

By the printed page as well as by oral transmission of Christian truth much was done to pave the way for pakeha settlement. The influence of Scripture teaching was one of the most potent that touched the life of the Southern native before European settlement became general. Having taught the Maori to read, Watkin had to meet a demand for literature. Supplies of the New Testament sent by the British and Foreign Bible Society reached him in April and again in September of 1843. Hearing of their arrival the natives gathered from miles around and almost stunned the missionary by their insistent demands for a pukapuka tapu (sacred book). They offered money, potatoes, firewood and treasured trinkets for the book above price.

One young woman was given a book and told that her ' man ' must pay for it.

' Oh,' she proudly replied, ' I will pay for it myself.'

She soon returned with a perforated half-crown that she had long prized and worn as an ear-pendant, and which probably four times its face value would not have tempted from her.

Many, taught in the mission schools, possessed the ability to read, and they followed with interest the Scripture lessons in the services for public worship. When catechized their pertinent answers pleased the missionary well. Their own inquiries about words, phrases and expressions were incessant, and those who had received Scriptural names in baptism were especially anxious to learn about the persons whose name they bore. Natives who obtained knowledge were anxious to pass it on to others. By oral communication a knowledge of hymns, prayers and catechism spread to every native settlement south of Moeraki by the middle of 1842. Night and morning in every village one could hear the sounds of song and prayer, the recital of the Commandments and the Apostles' Creed, and discussions on Christian doctrine and practice.

The native teachers who acted as pastors and evangelists also conducted schools for children and adults, but not the least of their contributions to Maori betterment was their example of orderly living and cleanliness, and their inspiration to active, useful life. So long as the Maoris remained heathen they showed no disposition to improve the outward conditions of life. They cared nought for better dwellings, well-tilled gardens, or the useful arts of the pakeha. But when a new force entered and brought a new hope they awoke immediately and in a manner altogether remarkable, to all the higher interests of life. Their unhappy lot was ameliorated. They were given a new sense of human worth and greatness, a loftier conception of the dignity of honourable industry and such a revelation of God and of duty as transformed the remnants of the native tribes into a healthy element in national development and accelerated the impulse that made possible the peaceable establishment of Scottish colonization and the steady development of the country in later years.

Chapter XIII

TRAVELS OF THE TRAIL-BLAZER

The road is rough and steep; to left and right,
Like ravenous beasts, lurk dangers that may fright
    E'en bravest heart;
I am not brave—a weakling at the best;
    Lord, strength impart!

The night is in my heart; its deadly murk
Is worse a thousandfold than sword or dirk
    That endeth all.
O Lord, in Thy great mercy let Thy light
Chase from my soul this dread enshrouding night
    Beyond recall.

—ROBERT FRANCIS.

No story of Otago would be complete that failed to take account of the travels of its pioneer preacher in doing his foundational work amidst acutest conditions. The natives amongst whom Mr. Watkin's work principally lay were few in number and scattered over a wide stretch of country from Moeraki as far south as Stewart Island. His health was not robust and often he was on the very verge of physical invalidism. Yet frequently he had to travel along the dangerous coast in canoes and crazy whaleboats manned by Maori lads, and sometimes to visit the Foveaux Straits and the regions beyond in any vessel available. Possessing no boat of his own, and having not the means to maintain a permanent Maori crew, he was forced to travel far afield on feet that were shackled with the chains of circumstance. Though a poor pedestrian at the best,

NO.	Date	Married	Residence	Witnesses names &c	By whom &c
		Marriage		Witnessed	
1	Jan 27/41	James Morvan Meri Fauru	Bluff	John Howell Elizabeth Howell Hannah Faithorn	James Watkin
2	June 19	Haimona Pita	Waikawaiti	Haimona Pita Mutu Pu Wrau Petri Horak	James Watkin
3	June 19	Reueni Emerene Hikuwa	Waikawaiti	maKai Emaira D Heitara Hohaia Mane Pohaitara	
4	June 19	Giare Petri Faihi Reuni Petri Mautara	Otakou	Kuje WeTari Piripa Petari Emma Metle Paihirohai	
5	April 19	Horemai Taharatham Roka Tahuna	Otako	Horemaia Taharaa Whun Poko Tahuna O Horomona Pokor	

THE FIRST ENTRIES IN THE FIRST MARRIAGE REGISTER USED
IN SOUTH ISLAND OF NEW ZEALAND. 1841.

Officiating Minister, the Rev. James Watkin, Wesleyan Missionary at he tramped many a weary mile, skirting swamps or wading cautiously through them ; fording rivers and climbing steep hills ; negotiating dense forests and ploughing through heavy sand-stretches. For a long period it was his practice to preach five times on a Sunday, thrice in Maori and twice in English. These services were held at Waikouaiti, Matainaka, Purakanui, Puketeraki, Otakou and elsewhere.

From the date of his arrival he gave considerable attention to Otakou and to the kaikas lying between his home and the peninsula. The moral conditions amid which the Maoris, especially at the Heads, lived their miserable, low-roofed life, wounded his heart to its depths. Let me describe a typical visit paid by Mr. Watkin to Otakou as gleaned from the pages of his Journal. He travelled thither in an open boat manned by a complement of five native lads. Only one of these proved an efficient boatman and the missionary himself took a turn at the oars, his very first experience of that form of exercise, and of the sport of ' crab-catching.' Twice on the way the boat was in danger of being swamped through shipping heavy seas. Having discharged his duties he desired to return to Waikouaiti, but, weather conditions proving adverse, he determined upon walking home, and of the journey he writes :—' It was long and tremendously fatiguing. The mountains are so steep that ascending and descending them is more fit for goats than for human beings. There are four rivers, or tide-ways to be negotiated. Crossing one of these took half an hour to effect, and most of the time I was up to the chest in water. A long and difficult swamp was one of the peculiarities of the road.'

Strictly speaking there was neither road nor track. Ploughing a passage through the swampy ground was a task aggravated by frequent stumbles upon the pukio, or ' niggerheads ' that there abounded. To the north of Koputai, the Port Chalmers of more modern days, was a dense undergrowth of labyrinthine briars and supplejacks.

I

The densely wooded hills above were an almost impene-
trable forest the negotiation of which was a formidable
task. This forest then extended along the foreshore and
far to the northward. There was many a thicket of flax
and fern through which the traveller had to thread his
path, and many a tearing tangle of villainous ' bush
lawyer ' that clung about the manuka and the mapau,
the fuchsia and the kowhai and other growths that then
abounded, through which he must win his forward way.
Fallen trees and steep, narrow gullies added to the toil-
someness of the journey. Through the woods the boom
of ocean surges sounded. Rolling mists now revealed
and now concealed the westering sun. The leaden heavi-
ness of dark clouds hanging overhead matched the mood
of his spirit when suddenly a rainbow reared its arch of
radiant hope athwart the blackest portion of the sky.
The noisy kaka kept up a chattering din. The weka sang
a duet with his mate. A feathered chorus tinkled and
trilled from leafy coverts when, with startling suddenness,
the voices of the woodland and the surge of the sea were
deadened by the roll of thunder that followed a blinding
lightning flash. Rain began to fall in torrents as he
emerged from the trees that stood like silent sentinels in
the encircling darkness in the vicinity of Purakanui, where
he accepted such shelter from the storm as was afforded
by a humble Maori whare. In this hut, only large enough
to accommodate two according to English notions, a dozen
people were crowded. The previous night at Otakou he
had been prevented by lack of room from spreading a
blanket, and now, wet and weary, he lay, or rather sat,
upon the earth floor in the fœtid atmosphere of the whare,
that was grimy and festooned with soot. There was little
chance to ' creep into the halls of sleep, and watch the
dreams go by.' Ere the mists had melted into morning
and the sun awoke the world, Mr. Watkin was astir.
Pursuing his way through the bush and the wet undergrowth he was soon saturated to the skin and ultimately

reached home stiff and exhausted, having slept little and eaten less during the period of his absence.

In barest outline let me now indicate the course of one of his later journeys. On December 12, 1843, he visited Otakou in a whaleboat with a crew of natives that included Rawiri Te Maire and Tiare Weteri Te Kahu. On the evening of that day he examined the candidates for baptism at Te Ruatitiko, a place situated beyond Taiaroa Heads. He also preached to and catechized the people and subsequently met the classes that he had put in charge of native teachers, and renewed the quarterly tickets of church membership to such as were enrolled. Next morning he married four Maori couples and baptized eleven adult Maoris and three of their children. He then passed to Tahakopa where he performed similar duties, holding one service indoors and another in the open-air. At these services he baptized thirteen adult natives and one Maori and three half-caste children. He also married four Maori couples and, much to his delight, four Europeans to the Maori women with whom they had been living in concubinage. Later in the day he visited Omate, near the Maori kaika at Otago Heads and there baptized three native women. He also married a Maori couple from Waipipiki afterwards proceeding to Tawhiroko that lay between the Heads and Koputai. Here he held evening service. He had purposed remaining for the night but found his lodgings so much alive with tuiau, or fleas, that he directed some of the boatmen to pull around to Waiparapara near the Spit whilst he and Rawiri Te Maire walked along the shore to that place, where they found shelter for the night. On the following morning they rowed to Purakanui under an almost torrid sun. Here two services were held. During the first service nine adult Maoris and seven of their children were admitted to the church by Christian baptism. Subsequently two native couples were married according to Christian usage. After the evening service Mr. Watkin, as usual in Maori quarters, found it impossible to court Nature's sweet restorer, so, at break of day, he took a walk on the sands until the morning was far enough advanced for holding a preaching service, after which he embarked and was rowed to Waikouaiti and the refreshing shelter of his own home.

To Moeraki, where Mr. Watkin very early established his work, and where some two hundred natives were dwelling in the early forties, he was a frequent visitor. Sometimes he travelled by whaleboat or canoe along the dangerous coast and felt the exhilarating taste of the brine upon his lips and the sting of it in his blood. Occasionally he journeyed on horseback, and once had occasion to remember his trip by being thrown from his mount. But usually he walked, in order that he might the better minister to several small Maori settlements along and off the usual route. This, involving as it did a tramp of some thirty miles each way, was a most fatiguing experience. In 1840 there was no well-defined track, and the walk was no small undertaking. It involved the climbing of steep ascents; the traversing of rolling downs covered with tussock, snow grass and toi-tois; the crossing of Teakapupu, that muddy estuary now known as ' Pleasant River '; the fording of frequent streams, which, like the Waihemo, or Shag River, ran through low and marshy land that had to be waded or otherwise negotiated; the tramp through the Ota-whata bush, a few miles south of the present Palmerston; the ploughing of stretches of sandy beach and the clambering of the rocky shore strewn with the famous Moeraki boulders around which science and romance have woven a fascinating story. Two places always included by the missionary in this trip were a fortified pa named Mata-kaea, situated at Shag Point, and a kaika that then stood to the north of that projection. The native village at Moeraki itself was on a promontory with a beach on either side, whilst behind it there lay a fine stretch of rich, well-watered, undulating country.

The drinking water at the village itself he found to be

so salt that he wondered how the natives could swallow it.
He could only account for their doing so by their love of
ease and their hatred of anything like avoidable work.
An interesting tradition giving the Maori explanation of
this extreme brackishness he chronicled during a visit
to Moeraki in March 1842, and as I have not met with
the tradition elsewhere I shall here put it on record.   It
appears that once upon a time an ill-behaved Maori youth
was going along the beach for some water when he saw
a whale that happened to be the vehicle of Takaloa, the
Lord of Ocean, who shares with Rona, the maid who sits
in the moon with a calabash at her side, the duty of controlling the tides of the sea.   The youth had the temerity
to shout to Takaloa one of the most offensive expressions
in Maori speech :—' To uboku faonaai.'   To this injunction
to Takaloa to ' boil his head ' was added the threat that
if he failed to obey, the youth would do it for him.   So
angered was his godship at this affront that he blew the
sea-water so high as to impregnate the springs at the top
of the mountain with the saline flavour they have retained
ever since !   I need scarcely explain that Takaloa is the
Southern form of Tangaroa, son of Rangi (Heaven) and
Papa (Earth), who is one of the great deities of Polynesia,
and was usually only seen in the misty spray of the sea
when the sun shone upon it.

Most of the Maoris at Moeraki were, from the first, very
ready to listen to the message of the missionary.   By oral
communication they had learned something of the hymns
and prayers and catechism he had taught at Waikouaiti.
They proved apt pupils when he paid his first visit of
instruction and were quick to erect a ' whare karakia,'
so that both Mr. Watkin and the native teachers he settled
among them might have a fit place in which to conduct
worship.   Often he was cheered, when, approaching the
settlement unseen by the Maoris, he heard sounds of
worship issuing from their dwellings as their voices were
raised in prayer and song, or as they chanted ' he katiki-

hama ' (the catechism) with great zest, and in tones which, though loud, were agreeable rather than otherwise. The hours of his periodical visits were crowded with duties. Each day he held two preaching services besides conducting sessions of the school. He dispensed medicine to the sick ; gathered the catechumens for instruction ; assembled the people both to catechize them and to answer their questions; baptized those qualified for Church membership and gave counsel and issued tickets of membership to those converts who were meeting each week in classes conducted by his native teachers. The Maoris crowded his services. Once, on Wednesday, September 27, 1843, there gathered a company so large that they adjourned to the open-air. Here, with the blue sky roofing Nature's grand cathedral and the green sward serving for fald-stool, nineteen adult Maoris and five children knelt to receive the sacrament of baptism. On the evening of the same day Mr. Watkin publicly set apart two young men to act as native ' leaders,' and later retired to his lodging in a dirty, smoky, flea-infested whare where sixteen fellow-lodgers were huddled into one apartment. Here his bed was the earth floor, his covering a blanket, his pillow a basket of potatoes which, at other times, served as his seat.

He was astir long before the eerie spirit of the night had sped on its course and the ghostly grey of the morning twilight had vanished at the rising of the red sun above the rim of the sea, whose plashing waves, creaming along the glistening sand, were soon to sing the sweet song of dawn. While waiting for the sleepy Maoris to muster for early morning worship ere he set out for Waikouaiti the air became aquiver with rapturous melody as

> Each lurking lyrist of the grove,
> With all his might, sang all his love.

But his thoughts were not of singing birds nor yet of triumphs already won among the heathen. He was brooding on the pitiful plight of many of the older people, still clinging tenaciously to their ancient deities and refusing to renounce the enslaving superstitions in which their souls delighted. For their conversion his heart was hungry. Hence neither the love notes of the tiheke, better known as the saddleback, the sweet minstrelsy of the koloheu, or New Zealand thrush, the gladsome mimicry of the tui or the friendly call of the flightless kakapo could silence the cry that for ever sang in his ears as he saw the Maori in his lostness and his need. Usually he was responsive to the overwhelming grandeur of creation, to the subtle splendour of manifold forms of life, the riot of colour in the landscape, and the solemn music of running brooks and rolling seas, and singing birds. In these things he had space to walk, to wonder and to worship. They lifted him above the petty thoughts and pursuing cares of a circumscribed life. But in the dark hours of depression, the delight he ordinarily experienced in the contemplation of the marvels of Divine architecture failed to induce in him

> That blessed mood
> In which the burthen of the mystery,
> In which the heavy and the weary weight
> Of all this unintelligible world
> Is lightened.

The beauty of Nature served, rather, to throw into bolder relief the ugly fact of sin that for ever flung itself into the foreground of his life.

But let us bear Mr. Watkin company by sea to the southward on a visitation to his stations in the regions bordering Foveaux Straits, where most of the natives were in vital fellowship with the Wesleyan Mission. Watkin had always felt a special interest in this locality. Through Foveaux Straits he had made his first approach to his New Zealand sphere of service. It was from this vicinity that there came to Waikouaiti, on January 27, 1841, the parties to the first Christian marriage ever celebrated in

Otago. This was an Anglo-Maori union between one
James Spencer and Meri Kauri of the Bluff. The couple
had come at the earliest opportunity that offered so that
their union might be hallowed by Christian rites. The
native woman also received Christian baptism immediately
before her marriage.

It was at Ruapuke, in this region, that Tuhawaiki, the
principal chief of the South Island, had his stronghold
and centre of influence, and here, naturally, that very deep
interest was manifested both by the chief and his people
in the advent of a missionary to their tribal domains.
The significance of that advent Tuhawaiki himself fairly
well realized. It was from Ruapuke that there came to
Watkin for Christian baptism some of the first-fruits of his
work.

The journey now to be described was one undertaken
during the last year of Watkin's term in Otago. To visit
Ruapuke and his other stations scattered on the coast
and islands thereabouts Mr. Watkin set sail in the schooner
Scotia from Waikouaiti on February 22, 1844. After a
night of buffeting by adverse winds and of battling against
a strong northerly current, the *Scotia* was compelled to
return to her anchorage to await favouring breezes. She
sailed again on February 24, reaching Taieri that night
to discharge cargo and disembark passengers. This done,
the schooner continued southward against persistent
adverse winds. She did not reach Foveaux Straits until
the night of the 27th, and darkness prevented her making
port. Next morning a strong ebb tide still impeded progress, and not until the morning of February 29 did they
gain anchorage in Bloomfield Harbour, as the Bluff was
then called.

Bad weather kept them at this place, but as most of the
Murihiku, or Southern Maoris, were Wesleyans, Mr. Watkin
busied himself in visiting and preaching to both the natives
and the Anglo-Maoris, of whom there were a good number,
and several of whom he baptized. The *Scotia* left her

A MOERAKI MAORI.

THE FAMOUS MOERAKI BOLDERS.

anchorage at the Bluff on the morning of March 3, and after a stormy passage across the Straits reached Stewart Island, where they dropped anchor at Kairakau, now known as Half Moon Bay. Here many natives had assembled from various parts and to them Watkin gave counsel and distributed books. Later he married two white men to their Maori mates and baptized their children. On the following day (March 5) he held an interesting service under the shade of the trees and baptized three young Maori men whose Christian knowledge and experience qualified them to receive that rite.

At the conclusion of the service the *Scotia* departed and by evening reached a place called Jacob's River. The native name of this place was Aparima, so-called after a woman of high degree in the Waitaha tribe probably seven centuries ago. Here the missionary met the assembled natives, conducted Divine worship, distributed books and visited a school that had recently been established for Anglo-Maori children and gave to the master such assistance as he could render. The anchorage at Jacob's River being very dangerous the master of the *Scotia* left as speedily as possible for Ruapuke. To visit this island had been the principal object of the journey of Mr. Watkin, hence he was bitterly disappointed to learn now that the anchorage at Ruapuke was unsafe for the schooner and reluctantly recognized that he could not in conscience urge the owner to endanger his vessel. He knew that the disappointment of his native teachers and of his many converts at Ruapuke would be as keen as his own, but philosophically resolved to attempt another visit as soon as practicable. For the present he had to content himself with sending a letter and a parcel to Solomon Pohio, his principal teacher at that place. After a weary journey he reached home on March 8. At every place of call he had preached his evangel, instructed the catechumens, baptized natives who had been taught by his Maori colleagues, visited their schools and officiated at a number of marriages.

James Watkin carried on his heart a constant burden of anxiety for the churches that, through his ministry, had sprung up from Moeraki to the southernmost parts of New Zealand, churches in the care of which he was assisted by some twenty-six native teachers, some of whom were far from competent. He felt that to cope with the demands of his district at least two more white missionaries were needed. From far and near Maoris were coming to Waikouaiti to attend the ' Karakia ' and to see for themselves the transformation wrought by the evangel in tribal life and in personal character. Many visiting natives returned to their own villages to tell the tidings of the power of the missionary message to uplift and to redeem. They told it, too, in such fashion as to constrain many a dusky friend and neighbour to forsake the old practices and themselves to repair to the missionary to hear the word more perfectly.

Success brought its embarrassments and created calls beyond Watkin's capacities for response. He clearly saw that their inarticulate needs were deeper than their uttered entreaties. Between his ideals and their attainments a startling hiatus yawned. To throw a bridge across the chasm was the task that made his days blood-tinctured as he plodded along the hard and solitary pioneer pathway.

CHAPTER XIV

THE PATH OF POMPALLIER AND THE TRAIL OF TAMIHANA

Keep heart, O Comrade ! God may be delayed
By evil, but He suffers no defeat ;
Even as a chance rock in an upland brook
May change a river's course ; and yet no rock—
No, nor the baffling mountains of the world—
Can hold it from its destiny, the sea.
God is not foiled ; the drift of the World-Will
Is stronger than all wrong. Earth and her years,
Down Joy's bright way, or Sorrow's long road,
Are moving toward the purpose of the skies.

FOR six months after his arrival at Waikouaiti the Rev. James Watkin stood as the solitary prophet of the Cross within the borders of the South Island of New Zealand. That lonely distinction was challenged in November 1840, for on the 7th of that month Mr. Watkin records :

' I am no longer alone in the field of this Island now.'

On that date he heard of the arrival at Banks Peninsula of a Roman Catholic Mission party led by Bishop Pompallier who had been appointed by Pope Gregory XVI as Vicar-Apostolic of Western Oceania, and some time previously had embarked upon his work under the protection of the King of France, and was now planting a Mission amongst the French emigrants who had located themselves at Akaroa.

A fortnight later Mr. Watkin records the arrival of the Roman Catholic Bishop in his ship, the *Sancta Maria*, at Otakou Heads. The Bishop was accompanied by a catechist, Brother Florentin, and by two priests, Father

Comte, who had acquired a passable knowledge of a Northern Maori dialect, and Father Pesant, who had just arrived from France. The Bishop has placed on record the presence of Mr. Watkin at Waikouaiti, and states that the Otakou natives had already ' received among them some native disciples of heresy,' and that they had been taught a short prayer and a canticle which they sang night and morning, and possessed little Protestant books such as their native catechists hawked all over New Zealand.

In his Journal Mr. Watkin throws further light upon the visit of Pompallier. He tells of the efforts of the Roman Catholic missionaries to ingratiate themselves with the Otakou natives by means of presents, expresses repugnance to this method of gaining converts, and himself refuses to adopt it. He says that the Bishop was much disappointed at finding the native population so small and notes that he expects the field will again be left to himself alone. That is indeed what happened so far as Otago was concerned, for Bishop Pompallier records that ' at the end of ten days they (the natives) knew the necessary truths of religion, made the sign of the cross and said Catholic prayers.' So he concluded his and his Church's connexion with the natives of Otakou by celebrating Mass in a large shed, after which he left for the North, lamenting that for lack of funds and missionaries he must for the future leave Otakou to the Protestants.

Before taking his final departure to the North, however, the Roman Catholic Bishop spent five or six days at Moeraki. He claimed in that brief space to have ' converted the people to the Catholic faith.' How he did this we learn from the private Journal of the pioneer Wesleyan missionary. Mr. Watkin says that the Bishop and his party produced some effect upon the Maori mind that was, however, as fleeting as the visit of the Bishop himself, and that this evanescent influence was gained by the bestowal of gifts, by dazzling vestments and ornate ritual, by disparaging the Wesleyan missionary's own plain dress and equally plain mode of conducting religious worship, and by telling the simple natives that Hine, the wife of Maui, one of their gods, whose main function appeared to be the perpetration of practical jokes and impish pranks, was none other than the Blessed Virgin Mary. The only condition for baptism imposed upon the natives by the emissaries of Rome was, says Mr. Watkin, ' to learn the Creed and the Ave by rote.' He adds ' I might baptize scores if such qualification only were required.'

After leaving Otakou and installing Father Comte at Akaroa, the Roman Catholic Church did not again enter the Southern field until the gold fever set in, save for occasional visits by Father Petitjean in the late 'fifties, and at that period Cardinal Moran records that ' there were no priests, churches or schools in the whole district,' and only about ninety Catholics in the entire Province, including a dozen or so in the city of Dunedin.

Wandering natives who had gained more or less Christian knowledge in the North, brought Christian doctrine, albeit not unmixed with error, to different parts of the South Island. One of these was a West Coast native named Taawao. He had been instructed in Christian truth by a Wesleyan of the Ngapuhi tribe from North of Auckland, and during a journey southward had brought to the natives at Port Levy and other settlements their first knowledge of Christianity. Taawao, who was subsequently baptized by the Rev. James Watkin as ' Rawiri Kingi,' and another native named Hohepa Korehi acted for a time as Wesleyan teachers at Port Levy. Hohepa, who was a typical Maori teacher, and did good service for his Church, was one of a band of travelling evangelists sent out from the exceedingly successful Wesleyan Mission that had been established by the Rev. Samuel Ironside at Cloudy Bay in December 1840. These teachers regularly visited all the native settlements on the East Coast of the South Island, bearing the knowledge of Christian truth.

Occasionally, roving Anglican teachers bearing no

official authority came to the southward. Mr. Watkin heard of the first of these in November 1840, and in January 1842, when visiting Moeraki, he found a native who could read and write a little, he having learned to the northward from another Maori who had received his Christian knowledge from natives connected with the North Island Anglican Mission.

It was not, however, until December 10, 1842, that the Anglican Church sent native emissaries into the Otago district. These Maoris, whom Mr. Watkin says were ' innoculated with High Church notions,' had the temerity to stigmatize the Wesleyans who had pioneered the field as ' unauthorized intruders.' Professedly acting under the authority of ' Te Harawira ' (the Rev. O. Hadfield), they sowed sad sectarian discord in Otago. They did their utmost to bring Mr. Watkin and the Hahi Weteriana (Wesleyan Church) into disrepute, and to damage both in the estimation of the natives, ' a thing,' says Mr. Watkin, ' that must please the Wicked One well.' These raw Maori youths, echoing the tones of their spiritual masters, derided the Wesleyans for being ' a little Church and a young one,' the very weapon Rome was then using in the North to discredit Anglicanism itself. These dusky emissaries, using the figure of the Church as the Bride of Christ, said that the Anglican Church was his true spouse, but the Wesleyan Church simply ' he wahine paremu ' (concubine).

Many an entry in the Journal of the noble Wesleyan pioneer, and many a passage in his letters to his colleague at Cloudy Bay, the Rev. Samuel Ironside, show how grieved was his spirit at the sad exhibition of intolerance, and at the persistent efforts to poison the minds of the natives against Methodism.

He writes :—' God forbid that the civil feuds of the Maoris should be succeeded by religious ones. My soul sickens at the thought of religious dissension among the natives. I would have them to be Christians and not sectaries.'

Again he exclaims :—' Bigotry is a cursed thing,' and he asks ' When will Catholic love prevail ? ' He prayed that God would forgive these sowers of strife whether they acted from ignorance or from malevolence, and in setting forth his own attitude, he says :—' It has been and will be my aim to instruct the natives in Christianity. Perhaps it may surprise, and I hope it may instruct, the emissaries of Te Harawira who come this way, when they see that I do not retaliate.'

That spirit of Christian magnanimity continued to mark Mr. Watkin in his later relationships with the Anglican Church and with Bishop Selwyn, to whom was attributable the early spread of sectarian bitterness in New Zealand. But to this we shall later return.

In the middle of January 1843 Matene Te Whiwhi, afterwards an influential chief on the West Coast of the North Island, paid a visit to Waikouaiti. He had been sent by the Rev. O. Hadfield in company with his cousin, Wiremu Tamihana, the only surviving son of the old warrior, Te Rauparaha, to tell the natives that the Wesleyan missionaries were not of the true Church. These vagrant teachers, who, for a few months, made an unfortunate intrusion into Otago, sowing the tares of intolerance, and branding the Wesleyans as schismatics, bore the imprimatur of their masters. They sought to make proselytes with more of the native than the Christian spirit, in ground that had, about Canterbury, been already covered by the preaching squads of the Rev. Samuel Ironside ; and in the South, in areas where Watkin and his Maori teachers had spread the truth ; teachers who, in defence of their own work were now forced into profitless discussion of sectarian questions.

Matene Te Whiwhi and Tamihana went on different ways, but with one objective. They managed to stir up strife at Pigeon Bay, Port Levy, Akaroa and Te-Wai-Ate-Ruate, near Temuka, and in the various Kaika as far south as Rakiura (Stewart Island), and indeed wherever Wesleyan teachers had carried the evangel.

Many garbled accounts of the visit of Tamihana have been given by partisan historians whose remarkable efforts to adorn a plain tale afford a truly delightful example of the growth of legend. The 'Tamihana Legend' was so effectively dealt with in 1902 by the Rev. P. W. Fairclough in his pamphlet, *The Early History of Missions in Otago*, that it has since cropped up only in ill-informed circles. In the year just mentioned the late Bishop Nevill claimed for Tamihana the honour of planting the Christian religion in Otago, an entirely fictitious claim. Canon Stack and others advance the utterly mythical contention that the work of Tamihana and Matene was rewarded by the conversion of the entire population, and say that for two years the son of savage old Te Rauparaha was in momentary peril of having 'utu' exacted from him by the Southern natives, to gratify hatred and in satisfaction of the ancient blood feud. It is significant, however, that neither Tamihana himself, nor Bishop Selwyn nor any of their contemporaries knew of any such peril. The best authorities deny that any risk at all existed, for the Maoris had already been Christianized by Watkin and Ironside and their agents long before Tamihana came to the South.

The supposition that Tamihana was in any peril was inferred from the fact that Tamihana's father, amongst his other exploits, had made terrible raids on Kaikoura, Kaiapoi and Akaroa in that troublous quadrennium 1828–1832. Te Rauparaha did not come farther south than Akaroa, although the Ngai-Tahu tribe, which he was assailing, extended to the extreme southward. Taiaroa, with the native braves of Otakou, had taken a heroic part in the defence of Kaiapoi, escaping shortly before the place fell. Twice Tuhawaiki and Taiaroa had led avenging forces to Cook Strait. Later, desiring peace, Te Rauparaha sent back the principal captives of war bearing peace offerings to the Southern chiefs, the rest of the prisoners of war remaining, meanwhile, as slaves. A treaty of peace was concluded and was thereafter faithfully observed.

A TYPICAL PIONEER HOME.

The healing of this ancient breach and the spread of Christian influence through the Wesleyan missionaries, made it perfectly safe for Tamihana to come to the South, particularly as he spent most of the time of his brief stay in the localities where his father had never penetrated.

Tamihana left in his track a legacy of sectarian strife that destroyed the sense of unity in many a pa. His chief ' successes ' were at Moeraki and at Ruapuke. At the former place Mr. Watkin had long had an organized branch of his mission, with classes for baptized converts conducted by native leaders. A chapel had been erected by the Maoris, and the natives were regularly summoned to worship by the beating of the kohua, that is, a round iron pot, such as is used in cooking.

Dr. Shortland, who visited Moeraki in November 1843, says that the natives, though mostly Christian, were divided into two parties, the children of Wesley and the children of Paihia, and that these maintained such constant religious disputes, that division and bad feeling had been introduced into almost every family, and that the two iron pots used for bells kept up a loud and obstinate rivalry. So far did this rivalry extend that even the prayers of the Wesleyan native teachers were not exempt from criticism. It was called ' Pokonoa,' that is, an unwarranted piece of presumption, for the Wesleyans to use extemporary prayers when even the Bishop read prayers from a book !

A few months after Dr. Shortland's visit to Moeraki the place was touched by the Rev. J. F. H. Wohlers, then in search of a field of labour, but he records that as the natives were already under Wesleyan care there was no opening for him. A few days previously Wohlers had refused to begin work at Port Levy as there were already native teachers there, and he was disinclined to drive a wedge between the two Wesleyan stations at Waikouaiti and Cloudy Bay. Upon that decision he later congratulated himself when he heard of the establishment of the Anglican Settlement in Canterbury. He had no sympathy

K

with the spirit that sent Tamihana to the South and said, ' I love Christianity as the Bible teaches it, which includes all disciples of Jesus, but I cannot bear to be in an exclusive Church coerced by human rules ! '

At Ruapuke, as a result of the visit of Tamihana, heathen communities had been divided by the introduction of the historical differences of older lands, and the Anglican converts had set up, beside the Wesleyan chapel, a humble building thatched with grass. Mr. Wohlers, who had, with the goodwill of the Wesleyan missionaries, found a sphere at Ruapuke in April 1844, tells how, through sectarian strife, ' there was no community of spirit, not even that of mere companionship,' and he records that when Bishop Selwyn paid his first visit, which was shortly before his own arrival at Ruapuke, that His Lordship had, in cynical contempt, dubbed the two conventicles by the name ' Babel,' and that the simple natives, not seeing the irony, had accepted the derisive appellation. At this period Mr. Watkin had many baptized converts at Ruapuke, together with resident native teachers, the principal one being Horomona Pohio, a well-known chief. Here he also had in training for the office of teacher Tione Topi Patuki, a converted chief who had borne a conspicuous part in the massacre at Tuturau in the year 1837.

Tamihana was at Waikouaiti on Sunday, July 9, 1843. On this date the congregations of the Rev. James Watkin, which for several weeks had been worshipping in the frame of the new church, then rapidly approaching completion, were so large that the missionary was compelled to take his stand out of doors. In the morning he preached from the text John iv. 24, and enlarged upon the nature of God and of the worship He requires. At the afternoon service prayers were read by Hohaia, from Ngakutu, one of the converts of the Rev. Samuel Ironside. Hohaia was a teacher gifted above the average and had been attached to the Waikouaiti Wesleyan Station. Mr. Watkin, with his customary Christian bigness of heart, asked

Tamihana, the Church Mission emissary, to speak. Tamihana responded to the request and dwelt upon the narrative of the rich man and Lazarus, to which Mr. Watkin afterwards made reference in his exhortation. The good missionary placed on record that he was pleased with the earnestness and humility of Tamihana, but he thought the Rev. Octavius Hadfield had something to answer for in endeavouring to poison the natives' minds against their fellow-Christians.

Leaving Waikouaiti, Tamihana apparently went southward, little dreaming how fateful were the events happening to his father. On August 10, 1843, Mr. Watkin received news from the Rev. S. Ironside of that fearful tragedy, the Wairau Massacre, that had occurred on June 17, a tragedy that would have been averted had the counsel of Ironside been heeded, and the pleadings of Rawiri Kingi Puaha, that noble Wesleyan chief and teacher, listened to, a tragedy that utterly wrecked the prosperous Wesleyan Mission at Cloudy Bay, and aggravated every missionary problem throughout New Zealand.

Although the Wairau Massacre had occurred three weeks before the date of Tamihana's visit to Waikouaiti, news of the tragedy travelled slowly southward. When at last it did reach Tamihana, he and his cousin Matene hastened homeward, as the slaughter of the survey party of the New Zealand Association threatened for a time to put upon Te Rauparaha, who was so intimately concerned with it, either the necessity for war, or the risk of the hangman's noose. Returning to Otaki, he was there, towards the end of 1843, confirmed by Bishop Selwyn, and when he later learned that Te Pihopa (the Bishop) contemplated visiting the south, he offered on January 1, 1844, to bear his Lordship company. This episcopal visitation and the relations of the Bishop himself to his Wesleyan fellow-Christians, yet remain to be dealt with.

Chapter XV

THE NARROW ARITHMETIC OF SECTARIANISM

Wast thou made much of words, and forms, and tests,
And thought but little of the peace and love—
His Gospel to the poor ? Dost thou condemn
Thy brother, looking down, in pride of heart ?
　　　Go thy way !—
Take Heaven's own armour for the heavenly strife,
Welcome all helpers in thy war with sin.
　　　　　　　　　—Dean E. H. Plumptre.

To understand the movement of events we shall need to
take a step backward and turn our faces northward.
Very shortly after Samuel Marsden, the Anglican Apostle
to New Zealand, began the Christian conquest of the Maori
in the year 1814, he recognized that the magnitude of his
missionary task was such as to place it beyond the capacity
of any one ecclesiastical organization to master. Himself
the son of Wesleyan Methodist parents, Marsden invited
his friend, the Rev. Samuel Leigh, the Methodist missionary
pioneer in Australia, to visit New Zealand and to share
in the enterprise of its evangelization. Leigh visited the
country in 1818 and then returned to England to lay the
proposal before his Church authorities, with the result
that on January 22, 1822, he returned to New Zealand
and began to lay the foundation of the Methodist Maori
Mission. Upon landing, the need for his work was everywhere manifest. He was offered tattooed Maori heads
for purchase, and saw human heads, just cut from living
bodies, sticking upon poles besmeared with blood and
brains, whilst cruel cannibals, in savage triumph over

their neighbours, were roasting and eating dead bodies on the beach.

The challenge of existing conditions fused the workers of both Anglican and Wesleyan missions into a fraternal fellowship. The dire need of the natives overshadowed all personal and ecclesiastical considerations, and the happiest relations subsisted between the representatives of both Churches. Thus it was fitting that when on August 16, 1823, the Wesleyans acquired their first Mission site at Whangaroa, it was Marsden who witnessed the deed of cession.

By mutual desire and with the approval of their governing bodies in England, the Anglicans and Wesleyans, so far as tribal conditions permitted, delimited their respective spheres of work, the Wesleyans taking the Waikato and the West Coast of the North Island, and later extending to Cloudy Bay and Otago ; the Anglicans taking the East Coast of the North Island and other specific areas. This arrangement did not determine the point of junction in Cook Straits, but in this field the Wesleyans, as in the South Island, established the first Mission Station. This was inaugurated by the Revs. J. H. Bumby and John Hobbs in June 1839, but as early as April 1836 another Wesleyan missionary, the Rev. William White, paid a visit to Queen Charlotte Sound when travelling in the brig *Martha* from Sydney to Hokianga.

Anglicans and Wesleyans looked upon each other as members of one body. They used the same forms of service, the Wesleyans employing John Wesley's revision of the Book of Common Prayer. They met together in Holy Communion, co-operated with the utmost heartiness, studiously avoided all occasions of rivalry, and, as need arose through native migrations or by the return of released slaves, freely transferred members from one Church to the other. In consequence many native Christian families had been baptized, part by Wesleyans and part by Anglicans, and all rejoiced in a common faith.

The conjoint labours of the two Churches, thus happily united in sympathy, in affection and in objective, had resulted in the taming to gentleness of erstwhile ferocious savages 'whose carnivorous appetites had been glutted with the flesh of human victims.' Ancient antagonisms were allayed, family feuds were forgotten, superstitions were exploded, ignorance was dispelled, and mutual sympathy was displacing a frigid unconcern for others. The native character was becoming grounded in Christian principles, and the unifying touch of Christ was welding Maori and pakeha into a fellowship in which distinctions of race and colour were obliterated, and the colonists were beginning to glimpse the shining ideal of a fraternity in which there would be exhibited a co-operation of all Protestants to promote the Kingdom of God within the borders of New Zealand.

Within the Wesleyan sphere there lived the great fighting chief of Kapiti and Otaki, Te Rauparaha, who boasted that he literally ' ate his way through ' from North to South of the country, and during whose ruthless and devastating career it is calculated that no less than 60,000 lives had been sacrificed. For some time this redoubtable warrior had been expressing a desire for a missionary to undertake work in his district. About the year 1839, however— that being the year in which the English Wesleyan Conference designated the Rev. James Watkin, who was then exercising a popular ministry in Sydney, for work at Kapiti—Te Rauparaha changed his mind and refused to facilitate the evangelization of his people.

Circumstances, however, circumvented the old chief. Released slaves from Church of England stations in the North had returned to their still heathen relatives in the vicinity of Te Rauparaha's headquarters. Bringing with them a knowledge of Christian truth, these liberated slaves influenced some of their kinsmen to look for missionary assistance to Paihia, the Anglican headquarters. They found a willing helper in Te Rauparaha's own son,

Tamihana, who, in spite of his father's opposition, boarded a whaler and went to the Bay of Islands, where he made his representation to the Anglican authorities and asked for a teacher. No teacher was, at the time, available. There was, however, a young cleric of some twenty-three summers, at the Mission Station. He had come to New Zealand with Bishop Broughton of Australia in H.M.S. *Pelorus* in December 1838, and was engaged in teaching European children, as he had not then acquired a knowledge of Maori. This young man was Octavius Hadfield who, some years later, became Commissary to Bishop Selwyn, and in 1870 became Bishop of Wellington. Hadfield's curiosity was aroused by the presence of Tamihana and he asked what the Maori was saying. On the representations of the native being translated to him he immediately offered his services. He was admitted to priest's orders and on October 21, 1839, left for Otaki, where he was inducted early in November by the Rev. Henry Williams.

As we have seen in an earlier chapter the appointment of Mr. Hadfield to Otaki involved an invasion, in breach of the existing compact, of territory that had hitherto been regarded as within the Wesleyan sphere. This departure from the traditional policy of the two Churches to work in friendly unity had other far-reaching consequences. It spread amongst a people lately emerged from savagery a lamentable spirit of ecclesiastical strife which not only operated in the direction of religious disunion, but later served to aggravate the tragedy of war between the Maori and pakeha races. Incidentally it disappointed many a missionary in both the Churches of the full harvest of his spiritual seed-sowing.

The action of Mr. Hadfield in going to Otaki, and thus leaving Mr. Watkin without his designated sphere marked the first departure from the spirit that had been fostered by good old Samuel Marsden, but the arrival in New Zealand on May 30, 1842, of Bishop Selwyn, was at once made the signal for spreading a discord that everywhere wrought irreparable mischief. The writer of Brett's *Early History of New Zealand* says of the Bishop :— ' The duty he conceived to be imposed upon him of establishing his Church throughout the colony caused him to refuse recognition to the Wesleyans as a co-ordinate Christianizing missionary body.'

He viewed with stern disapproval the brotherliness that prevailed amongst Wesleyans and Anglicans, and immediately sought to sever the happy fellowship, alike by intolerance of action and exclusiveness of tenet. One of his earliest acts was to secure and consecrate separate cemeteries, so that, after life's fitful fever, deceased Anglicans might lie apart from dead ' dissenters.'

There is little profit in raking the ashes of ancient controversy and positively no pleasure in sitting in the seat of the critic when the actions of great and good men are in question. It is so easy, in aiming at truth, to miss charity, and in rebuking arrogance to betray a spirit utterly alien to the meekness we extol. But, as the ecclesiastical misunderstandings that became general with the advent of Bishop Selwyn had their effect upon the work of evangelizing the natives of Otago and South-land, and also helped to shape the larger history of our land, necessity compels one to touch upon them, albeit with as gentle a pen as one may justly wield. It is both foolish and futile to attempt to veil vital differences in verbal ambiguities, for truth, when told with kindly candour, is ever an instrument of peace and goodwill.

When speaking with one of his own biographers Selwyn himself said :—' Tell first all my faults, and then tell whatever the grace of God has enabled me to do in spite of them.' If, in this narrative, I first pay a sincere tribute to his transcendent merits, freely confessing his genuine love for the Maori, his amazing zeal and tireless industry, and then refer to the circumstances that led so kindly a critic as the Rev. W. J. Williams to ask why it is that

A MAORI SWING.

(From an old wood-cut in the 'Wesleyan Missionary Notices.')

the Bishop 'moves across the scene of missionary history in New Zealand as the man who, nearly everywhere, casts a shadow,' I shall ask that the limitations of His Lordship be viewed in the light of his conspicuous virtues.

George Augustus Selwyn was undeniably a great and good man. In him were embodied some of the finest elements of English breeding and culture. To view him through the curtain of his faults and foibles is like contemplating a splendid landscape through a smoked glass. One sees then but a blurred and inadequate image of the object of vision. Selwyn was, as the author of *Centenary Sketches of New Zealand Methodism* says, 'a man of high character, of deep piety, of lofty aim, of splendid courage, of great administrative gifts and of absolute devotion to what he conceived to be his duty.' He was young, self-willed and self-confident and fired with a passion to fashion the Church in New Zealand after the High Church pattern. Finding that the Wesleyan Missions were the chief obstacle in the path to that pre-determined goal he dismayed the older Anglican missionaries, and at the same time gave joy to his Roman Catholic critics who branded all Protestants equally as heretics and impartially excommunicated both the Anglican and the Wesleyan 'schismatics.' The fact is that Bishop Selwyn was hag-ridden by indefensible ecclesiastical theories that led him to provide many an occasion for the scorner to exclaim 'Alas for the rarity of Christian charity under the sun.' Rarely has so good a man been the instrument of such great and tragic mischief.

Although the very safety with which the Bishop could move about in an erstwhile cannibal country was due, in large measure, to the influence and teaching of devoted Wesleyan missionaries, so disdainful was he of them and their wonderful work, that, on October 31, 1843, he wrote to the Wesleyan District Committee, composed of men who, for varying periods, had exercised a gracious and fruitful ministry amongst the Maoris, telling them,

with more candour than courtesy, that Wesleyans were
schismatics, that their ordinations were invalid, and that
their baptisms at most were acts of mere laymen.

At the Bay of Islands, where the Maoris were under
the spiritual oversight of that distinguished Wesleyan
missionary and translator, the Rev. John Hobbs, the
Bishop told the astonished natives that the 'orders' of
the missionaries who had won them from heathenism were
irregular, that he, as Bishop, was their head, and the
schismatic Wesleyans merely the feet. This sapient
sentiment drew from a converted chief the very significant
and warning rejoinder :—

'Then, Bishop, don't cut off your feet, or your head will
be of little value.'

The ecclesiastical exclusiveness that led Selwyn to refuse
to address the clergy of other Churches, either in speech
or by pen, by the mere courtesy title of 'Reverend,' and
that prompted him to tell the Rev. Thomas Buddle,
another notable Wesleyan, that he did not recognize the
ministerial status of non-episcopal missionaries, brought
upon him many a rebuke from the lips of quondam
cannibals.

Te Awaitai, the great Whangaroa chief, faithful friend
of the pakeha, and one of the most celebrated natives of
modern Maori history, who is better known as Wiremu
Nera (William Naylor), speaking in 1845 at a public
function in the presence of Governor FitzRoy, of the work
the Wesleyans had done to win him and his people from a
horrible heathenism, lamented the denominational division
that had been introduced, and complained that his people
were being told that the Wesleyans were slaves and the
Anglican chiefs, that the steps of Wesleyans tended to
hell and the steps of Anglicans to heaven.

Selwyn traversed the West Coast of the North Island,
the Wesleyan sphere of influence and activity, astonishing
the natives by declaring that the Wesleyans were 'a
crooked branch,' and 'a fallen people,' and that they had

no Scriptural ministers. Taking their cue from their
master some of Selwyn's clergy pressed into the Wesleyan
Mission Stations making the sign of the Cross on the
foreheads of foolish natives ' to make their baptism
complete.'

The Bishop coveted for the Anglican Church Epiha
Putini (Jabez Bunting), the influential Waikato chief, of
whose baptism by the Wesleyans he had been informed.
Aware of Putini's grief that the Wesleyan Church would
send no ' chief ' to his tribe the Bishop himself approached
the chief and offered to send him a clergyman provided
he would accept re-baptism and enter the Anglican
Church through an episcopal administration of that
sacred rite.

' Pihopa,' said the chief, ' how often was Jesus
baptized ? '

' Once,' confessed the Bishop.

' Then,' replied Putini, with courteous and chiefly
dignity, ' once will do for me.'

It was inevitable that painful results should everywhere
follow Selwyn's reversal of the former attitude of his
Church, but the most lamentable effects of his insensate
policy were produced amongst the native population.
The Bishop had egregiously miscalculated the native
character, and the tragic results issuing from his error
were set forth in courteous and graceful phrase in three
open letters to His Lordship, from the pen of that cultured
Wesleyan missionary, the Rev. H. Hanson Turton, of
New Plymouth. These were published in the Auckland
Southern Cross about May 1844. Mr. Turton, speaking
with that fulness of knowledge not yet acquired by the
Bishop, reminded Selwyn that already he had interrupted
the peace and endangered the security of a colony then
comparatively at rest, and warned him that his policy
amongst a people naturally proud, resentful and sanguinary, was fraught with gravest danger, inasmuch as
the overbearing spirit that exclusiveness was sure to

infuse, would provoke insults that might lead to retaliation and bloodshed.

Mr. Turton's fears proved all too well grounded. Many an unconverted Maori, seeing that the Bishop's attitude to his fellow Christians looked a veritable ' twin of heathen hate,' was moved to declare that ' heathenism with love is better than Christianity without it.'

Under the former regime it frequently happened that part of a family had been baptized by Wesleyans and part by Episcopalians. The new policy resulted in mortal hatred springing up between parents and children. The life of many a pa was split in twain. Former friends would neither sit, nor eat, nor commune together. Pas were sub-divided by fences that Anglican eyes might not light upon Wesleyan relatives, and upon one specific occasion, so high did feeling run between contending factions, that but for the timely action of a Wesleyan missionary, the Rev. J. S. Skevington, a scene that began with intolerance would have ended in blood.

CHAPTER XVI

BISHOP SELWYN'S SOUTHWARD EXCURSION

> It is the little rift within the lute
> That by and by will make the music mute,
> And, ever widening, slowly silence all ;
> The little rift within the lover's lute,
> Or little pitted speck in garnered fruit,
> That, rotting inward, slowly moulders all.
> —TENNYSON.

EARLY in 1844 Bishop Selwyn paid his first visit to the South Island. His biographer has recorded the distress the proud spirit of the Bishop experienced to find that everywhere he had been preceded by the Wesleyans. After touching at Akaroa he proceeded by stages to the extreme south. Everywhere he found instructed natives who were able to read, to recite the Lord's Prayer, the Apostles' Creed and portion of the Catechism. On January 13, at Te-Wai-a-te-Ruati, the old Maori pa near Temuka, he found traces of division between Wesleyans and the natives influenced by Tamihana and other Anglican propagandists.

Proceeding to Moeraki, at which place he had been preceded both by the Roman Catholic prelate, Bishop Pompallier, and by the Rev. James Watkin of the Wesleyan Mission, he baptized four natives on January 20 and then went on to Waikouaiti, where, for two days, he was the guest of the Wesleyan missionary. The Journals and letters of both the Bishop and Mr. Watkin give many details concerning this visit. Mr. Watkin writes that on January 23 he was much surprised and equally pleased with a visit from Bishop Selwyn, who was accompanied by several native youths, including Tamihana. Watkin had been told that Selwyn was a close, incommunicative man, but states that he found him the reverse of that. Of the Bishop, Mr. Watkin says ' He is, I suppose, the most primitive Bishop of the Church of England at the present time. He is in labours more abundant, in journeyings often. He is an excellent traveller, and can bear privations and endure exertions which would finish some of us who are below him in station. He appears to be as Catholic as can be expected in a person who believes as he does. He laments disunion. So do I. He wishes for unity. So do I ; but I see not how the unity he desires can be brought about. . . . May God bless him.'

Writing to his friend, the Rev. Samuel Ironside, Mr. Watkin said :—

' I admire him (Selwyn) on many grounds, but differ from him on many. We conversed on many topics, agreeing and differing. The Bishop is anxious for union. I mentioned a union of love. That is hardly it. He would dearly like all to belong to the Church of England. He is ignorant of us, and of our Founder and his writings. I think he is a good man as far as his prejudices will allow. I pray God to make him a blessing.'

The true spirit of Christian charity that marked the attitude of Mr. Watkin to the Bishop was further manifested in the gracious compliment he paid to Selwyn of asking him to catechize the natives of the Wesleyan Mission Station. The two men bade one another farewell, and the Bishop, as a memento of his visit, gave to Mr. Watkin a copy of St. Matthew's Gospel in Maori. It was one of an edition that had been given to him before he left England, and which he freely distributed to the Maoris he met so long as the supply lasted. The fly-leaf bore the inscription.

JAMES WATKIN,
With the best wishes of
G. A. N. Zealand.
Waikouaiti, 23 January, 1844.

From Waikouaiti the Bishop passed on to Otakou, where Watkin had his teachers, and where, from the meagre population, he had seventy-one natives enrolled in Church membership. Here, to Watkin's surprise, the Bishop planted a native teacher whom he had baptized a few days previously at Moeraki. Well pleased with this piece of work the Bishop sailed for Foveaux Straits, arriving at Ruapuke on January 28. Here the Wesleyans had a number of baptized members, including some of the chiefs, and a class of some twenty natives who were able to read. The Bishop found, also, the strife that was usual as a result of Tamihana's brief visit of some months previously. He spent a fortnight in the Straits and everywhere found natives with knowledge of the art of reading, fairly well instructed in Christian truth, and mostly in fellowship with the Wesleyans. This condition was a notable outcome of Mr. Watkin's arduous labours.

Mr. Watkin, who went to the Straits soon after Selwyn's visit, records that the Bishop's coming had caused a little temporary excitement, but had not proved so productive as His Lordship had hoped. During their interview at Waikouaiti Mr. Watkin had proposed that in the interests of unity amongst the natives those who had attached themselves to the Church of England might be placed under the pastoral care of the Wesleyan missionary and his staff of native leaders, which then numbered twenty-six in the district stretching southward from Moeraki. To this the Bishop had given a positive refusal. Watkin, ever concerned more with promoting the kingdom of God than the welfare of a denomination, hearing of Selwyn's intention to place a missionary, whose life 'must be amphibious,' in the Foveaux Straits district, where most of the Maoris were Wesleyans, wrote to his trusty friend, the Rev. Samuel Ironside, stating that he was debating whether in view of Selwyn's determination, he should withdraw the Wesleyan teachers from the Straits and that region, and give up the Wesleyans to Anglican care.

Of this southern visit, the Bishop wrote to the Rev. O. Hadfield, in February 1844, a letter that is full of self-revelation. The Rev. H. W. Tucker, M.A., one of Selwyn's biographers, says that this letter, which he quotes with much approval, ' has special significance as showing that he (the Bishop) declined to recognize the mere presence of a Dissenting teacher in a given district as proof that that district was under Christian instruction.'

In Selwyn's view Watkin's work was ' irregular.' It mattered not that it was Watkin who first unfurled the banner of the Cross in the South Island of New Zealand ; that he stood at the centre of a real religious awakening ; that his work not only won outcast pakehas from animalism and vice, but also transformed heathen cruelty into love ; lit dusky Maori faces with the light of God, and sent erstwhile cannibals into the valley of the shadow of death with Christian hymns upon their lips and Christian hopes in their hearts. He was merely a ' dissenting teacher,' and as such the Bishop could not recognize his presence in the district as proof that it was ' under Christian instruction.'

It is little wonder that the Rev. P. W. Fairclough says of the Bishop's letter :—

' I think it would have been discreet in Selwyn's biographer to have suppressed this letter. It was written after weeks of humiliation to a proud spirit. As his biographer remarks, " Dissent has spoiled the pleasure of the trip." It is carping, ungenerous and self-excusing to a degree.'

The Bishop's letter, besides the significance claimed for it by Mr. Tucker, is remarkable for its confession that the good-hearted youth Tamihana ' is not very adroit in controversy and sometimes a little overbearing,' and also for the statement that Mr. Watkin had for three years been left by his Missionary Society with only one Testament, and that a few months ago his Committee had ' sent him down a flood of 500 Testaments.'

The fact is that while Mr. Watkin was often lamentably short of proper equipment, he received in December 1841 a book of instruction he had specially prepared for the Press a year previously, that from Mr. Ironside and others he received copies of the Testament, and that on April 28, 1843, he received a consignment of Testaments which led him to exclaim ' Kapai rawa ' ; and again on September 12 of the same year he was gladdened by the arrival of a case of Testaments, completing, with the former consignment, the allocation of 360 copies that was his share of a parcel of 10,000 books presented to the New Zealand Missions by the British and Foreign Bible Society.

The Rev. James Watkin, it need scarcely be said, never had any qualms about the validity of his own ' orders.' Although no episcopal fingers had touched his head, because he had deliberately refused tempting offers to enter the Anglican in preference to the Wesleyan ministry, he felt that his sanction was higher than that of episcopal ordination. His commission was authenticated, not by succession through historic sources, nor by transmission through any particular piece of mechanism, but by the call of God, by the recognition of the living Church, and by the attestation furnished in a fruitful ministry. The logic of facts in a wealth of transfigured lives, not only revealed that sacramental grace and spiritual power existed in full force outside episcopal boundaries, and that his was a true ministry endorsed with the signature of Divine approval, it also showed that the traditional theory of apostolic succession, conferring exclusive spiritual prerogatives, was a ludicrous anachronism.

It is practically certain that Bishop Selwyn himself regretted, upon reflection, the ill-considered intrusion of his proselytizing natives into a field already occupied. It is significant that, in his second episcopal visitation of the South there is no record of any visit to the Maoris. The Anglican effort in Otago was confined, so far as the

Maoris are concerned, to the brief attempt of native teachers and the one visit of their chief pastor. It may be added, too, that when the first resident Anglican minister, the Rev. J. A. Fenton, came to Otago, by appointment of Bishop Selwyn, in January 1852, he found, as he later placed on record, that the Anglicans here had ' no clergyman, no building, no land, no money.' Colonial life did much to emancipate the Bishop from the trammels of ecclesiasticism. As evidence that he outgrew some of his earlier prejudices, and softened in courtesy, let it be told to his credit, that during his later years in New Zealand, he refused to consecrate some of the remote country churches so that Wesleyan preachers would not be excluded therefrom. Again, when administering the Holy Communion at his last function in St. Matthew's Church, in Auckland, before his return to England, when he noticed the presence of two Wesleyan missionaries—the Rev. John Hobbs, and the Rev. James Wallis—the Bishop stepped aside and handed them the sacred emblems with the words ' May we meet again at the marriage Supper of the Lamb.' That act reveals the real Selwyn freed from the fetters of an indefensible intolerance. It proclaims too, the truth that the sundered units in the Christian Church will come together, by seeking, in the prayer chamber and at the Lord's Table, where all men are equal, such a baptism of the spirit of Jesus as will lift them above all petty prejudices and pre-suppositions.

An injustice would be done to the memory of Bishop Selwyn if one failed to acknowledge that he honestly believed in the mystical character of the episcopate as the one channel through which grace could be transmitted or the sacraments be effectively administered. Although not a film of evidence to support his view could be extracted from either the New Testament, the writings of the earliest Church Fathers, or the beliefs of the early Church, Selwyn allowed himself to be dominated by the assumption that the Apostles received a specific commission of authority, with power to transmit it, and that they made definite rules for episcopal ordination. Despite the fact that Archbishop Whateley, of Dublin, a contemporary of Selwyn, affirmed that no minister in Christendom could trace his spiritual pedigree back to the Apostles, Selwyn had a simple faith in the doctrine of an uninterrupted apostolic succession. Such a succession John Wesley, himself a priest of the Anglican Church, had long before declared to be a fable which no man ever did or ever can prove.

Happily the world has moved since Selwyn first came to Otago, for, though the doctrine of the Divine right of Bishops still lingers in some quarters, prelatical pretensions are no longer defended. So shrewd a critic as Dr. Inge, the Dean of St. Paul's, in a plea to his own people to ' repudiate decisively the pitiful theory ' that sunders Anglicans from their fellow-Christians, not only denies that they are ' the privileged courtiers of the Almighty, possessing a monopoly of magical power to give efficacy to the distribution of God's indispensable grace ' but he ridicules the notion ' that Bishops are invested with any supernatural gifts ' or possess any ' supernaturally guaranteed wisdom.' Another Anglican, Dr. Headlam, Regius Professor of Divinity at Oxford, and one of the most eminent scholars in his Church, rejects the dogma of Apostolic succession, as he holds the evidence is all against it. The Bishops, too, at the 1920 Lambeth Conference, had a sublime vision of a united Church, a vision that can be hailed as the prophecy of a better day, although its realization can only yet be saluted from afar. They acknowledged ' the spiritual reality of the ministries which do not possess the episcopate,' and they frankly declared that the membership of Methodists and other Christians equals their own in the Universal Church of Christ. When Christian people of every name come to recognize that all denominations are but incidents in the growth of the Kingdom of God, and that the great central fact is the One

Church of the Divine Lord, we shall achieve such a unity as will give to the Christ that body which will prove to be the effective instrument through which He can save and renew a suffering and distracted world.

CHAPTER XVII

RECORDS OF THE RANGATIRAS

And when across the arch of night
The moon wings forth in radiant flight,
Do ghostly whalers sail the bay
And ghostly crews make holiday
With ribald mirth, to drink or sup
Or set a phantom try-pot up ?
Do shades of Natives ever come
To barter pigs for nails and rum
And dusky nymphs disport them still
About the bows of ' Gange ' or ' Nil ' ?
—MONA TRACY.

THE sort of mental trellis on which the pioneer missionary made the flowers of the Spirit to grow may be gathered, so far as the masculine constituency of Southern Maoridom is concerned, from a glance at some of the outstanding men who made native history in the flaming years before the Scottish Settlement. Some were chiefs and priests among their people and not a few of these became teachers in the Wesleyan Mission. Included amongst those with whom Watkin had close fellowship were the warriors who, armed with muskets, formed the party of retaliation at Tuturau in 1837. These included Tuhawaiki, whose authority was supreme, Tione Topi Patuki, who was next in rank, Taiaroa, Haereroa, Hape and other prominent native figures.

Tuhawaiki was popularly known as ' Bloody Jack.' This appellation was not the outcome of his bloodthirsty disposition, but was conferred because of his frequent use of the sanguinary adjective that he had picked up from the whalers. An illustration in this volume reproduces the moko signature, or face tattoo, of this distinguished rangatira as it was drawn by himself on December 31, 1835, on a deed confirming a sale of land by his old uncle to one Peter Williams. When the agreement to sell 400,000 acres for the Otago Settlement was completed on June 20, 1844, it was signed by Tuhawaiki, Karetai, Taiaroa and twenty-two other chiefs. The purchase price was £2,400. When the money was paid at Koputai on July 31, 1844, Tuhawaiki received £900 together with an additional £300 for division among his connexions. The minor chiefs, Karetai and Taiaroa, got £300 each, and the remaining £600 was divided among the other chiefs and the Otakou Maoris.

Tuhawaiki was born at Tau-hinu, now known as Inchclutha. His father's name was Kaihaere and his uncle was that notorious old cannibal warrior, Te Whaka-taupuka, who, amongst other things, was remarkable for the possession of six toes on each foot, a characteristic that also marked Tuhawaiki's own son, Kehu. Te Whakataupuka disappeared from Southern Maori history in 1835, a victim to the epidemic of measles that decimated the native population in that year. He was succeeded by his handsome young nephew, Tuhawaiki, who thereafter became the dominating figure in Southern Maoridom. The young chief was the idol of the remnants of the conquered tribes of the south and his influence extended from Ruapuke to Port Cooper, which is the Lyttelton harbour of to-day.

In the ten years preceding the coming of the Wesleyan missionary Tuhawaiki had shared in or organized many a war-like expedition, most of them directed against the famous Ngatitoa chief, Te Rauparaha, in revenge for outrages perpetrated by that notable northern warrior and his braves. Tuhawaiki it was, who led the party that committed the historic massacre on the banks of the

Mataura River in 1837, when many of the northern marauders were killed and eaten, and others were taken as slaves to Ruapuke, including one whose ears had been cut off by Tuhawaiki himself.

The stronghold of this chief and his hapu was at Ruapuke, a small island in Foveaux Straits, and an influential centre of Maoridom, having in 1844 a population that numbered 200 souls. Tuhawaiki was above middle height, well proportioned, handsome and intelligent. He had a remarkable memory and possessed a wide knowledge of the geography of the South Island. Long before the pakeha discovered gold Tuhawaiki told the whalers that there was plenty of the precious metal on the banks of the Matau, better known as the Molyneux River. He had a reputation for integrity and straightforwardness. Mr. Watkin recorded his judgement that Tuhawaiki was superior to most of his countrymen but had been brutalised by his intercourse with Europeans.

During a visit that Tuhawaiki paid to Sydney he had been presented by Governor Gipps, that good friend of the Maoris, with several old military suits. Tuhawaiki therefore formed a bodyguard of six native soldiers arrayed in British uniforms minus headgear and footwear. In charge of the squad he placed a uniformed orderly sergeant who had visited the Sandwich Islands and there gained some little military knowledge. Mr. Watkin describes a visit paid to Waikouaiti on October 19, 1840, by the great chief, his bodyguard, and as many of his people as four large boats could carry. Tuhawaiki himself was resplendent in the full dress staff uniform of a British aide-de-camp, with gold lace, trousers and cocked hat. He carried himself with a fine military air, and, says Mr. Watkin, ' might not be ashamed of standing alongside the first military dandy nor he of him.' The sergeant put his squad through its drill, upon which the missionary wrote the comment that it was ' rather a ludicrous scene to people who have witnessed the evolutions of European troops, but no doubt an imposing spectacle to native eyes.'

This party had come from Ruapuke to the Mission headquarters at Waikouaiti largely because of their anxiety to hear the strange, new message that the missionary was now eloquently proclaiming in their own tongue. On this day many heard for the first time truths that pierced the opaque depths of life. Instinctively they felt that in Watkin was one who could unsnarl their perplexities, and they felt little resentment that through him myths grown hoary were being cast into eternal exile.

Waikouaiti was a central rendezvous for the scattered Maoris of Te Wai Pounamu. On June 4, 1842, large fleets of canoes arrived there from the north and from the south at the height of a violent storm blowing from the north-east. They brought a great crowd of natives to hold a korero with Tuhawaiki. One of these natives delivered to Mr. Watkin from Tuhawaiki a note written on a slate requesting a bottle of brandy. Mr. Watkin replied that he did not possess such a thing and would not give it if he had it.

Other business transacted, Tuhawaiki asked Mr. Watkin to send a European missionary to reside at Ruapuke. A fortnight later he came to renew the request and promised that if one were sent, the people would attend to his instructions, but he raised strong objections to Ruapuke having to put up indefinitely with native agents who were necessarily somewhat incompetent.

On October 8, 1842, during a visit Mr. Watkin paid to Otakou, Tuhawaiki, who was there, again preferred his request for a missionary. Later in the day the fleet of the rangatira and the boat of the missionary came on to Waikouaiti and that night Mr. Watkin preached to a large company of visiting and local Maoris, including the chief, on the subject of Christ and Nicodemus. Nevertheless the request of Tuhawaiki was not forgotten, for when, in April 1844, the Rev. J. F. H. Wohlers came south in

THE MOKO SIGNATURE OF TUHAWAIKI, 1840

quest of a field of labour, Mr. Watkin, as we shall see in a later chapter, facilitated his settlement at Ruapuke.

Tuhawaiki, who had survived many a warlike encounter, met his death by drowning at Timaru on July 31, 1844. While standing at steer oar, piloting a boat through a tempestuous sea, he was struck by a big wave, swept overboard and perished. His son, Kehu, by a strange coincidence, also met his death by drowning whilst endeavouring to cross Foveaux Straits in a whaleboat during a gale of wind.

Among the prominent leaders of Southern Maoridom, there were few more striking figures than Te Matenga Taiaroa, the famous fighting chief of Otakou. He had many contacts with the missionary, but whilst most of his fellow-chiefs early joined the Wesleyan Mission, it was not until April 3, 1859, that he was received into the membership of the Methodist Church. On that date he was baptized by the Rev. George Stannard, and on the same day was married, according to Christian usages, to Karoraina, who belonged to the Ngai-te-ruahikihiki hapu, which was an offshoot of the Ngai-Tahu tribe.

Taiaroa himself sprang from the old fighting race of chiefs, and his name must always find a place in the tales of Southern Maoridom. He belonged to the Ngatimoki hapu of the Ngatimamoe tribe and was subordinate to Tuhawaiki. Judging from contemporary references he was not of prepossessing appearance. D'Urville, who was visited by Taiaroa on board the *Astrolabe* early in 1840, describes him as clad in rags, exhibiting insatiable greed and showing himself more in the light of a skilful rogue than as a chief of warriors. Mr. Tuckett, the surveyor, described him as ' an uncivilized Maori of marked but repulsive Jewish physiognomy.' Dr. David Monro also commented upon his Jewish cast of features, and gave an unflattering verbal portrait of him as an importunate beggar, dressed in a blanket and addicted to rum drinking. The Rev. James Watkin was not favourably impressed with him. Taiaroa often expressed a desire for Mr. Watkin to procure a white missionary for Otakou, a desire, Mr. Watkin judged, prompted by the ambition to be equal to his Waikouaiti neighbours in that regard, and by the fancy that his begging propensities might find exercise and gratification at a local mission house. Taiaroa was of middle height and possessed of prodigious strength, which became the servant of a most tyrannous and avaricious disposition. His avarice has been described as ' a keen sense of trade values,' and his robbing raids as ' the observance of the Maori code of muru or confiscation.' His deeds in the inter-tribal wars of the period are told in another chapter.

Taiaroa had no love for the Europeans and would have exterminated them if he could. On several occasions during the stay of Mr. Watkin at Waikouaiti he made threatening raids upon the Europeans there until Tuhawaiki warned him that if he interfered with the pakeha again he would bring the men of his own hapu to Otakou and terminate Taiaroa's own career. Prior to this effective threat Taiaroa, who had a wholesome dread of firearms, fled on at least two occasions when his raids upon Waikouaiti settlers were met with armed resistance. On another occasion when the American brig *Pearl* could not, through stress of weather, get out of Otago harbour, Taiaroa, aspiring to capture her, mustered his canoes for that purpose. Finding the ship prepared for attack he deemed discretion the better part of valour and temporarily retired. Meanwhile a party from the *Pearl* had secretly landed. Catching Taiaroa they put him in irons and kept him prisoner until the vessel cleared the Heads, and then landed him on the rocks, leaving him to walk home, a sadder and a wiser man.

After the Wairau massacre in 1843, when the white settlers were fearful for their safety, Te Rauparaha endeavoured to gather to his standard his ancient enemies of the South. With this end in view he proposed an alliance and in proof of his goodwill sent home to their tribe a number of prominent prisoners. After earnest deliberation the olive branch was accepted, and in token of the healing of the breach Taiaroa visited Te Rauparaha at Kapiti and assured him of the future friendship of the Southern Maoris.

In his later years Taiaroa set apart ten acres and built a church on this area at Otakou. The building cost £150, of which sum the Government provided one third. The old chief lived for four years after publicly accepting Christian baptism, and was buried on February 17, 1863. Before his death he counselled his descendants to live at peace with the pakeha and to observe their undertakings.

Another notable chief to whom reference has already been made was Tione Topi Patuki, who, after his conversion, became a Wesleyan teacher at Ruapuke. When the survey of Foveaux Straits was being carried through by Captain Stokes, Topi rendered admirable service by his intimate knowledge of those regions. This chief lived until he was about ninety and passed away on October 1, 1900.

Karetai, also known as ' Jackey White,' was another influential chief of the 'forties. He had a number of slaves and four or five wives. One wife was Hini Pakia, a son of whom was baptized by the Rev. William Kirk on March 19, 1854.

Rawiri Waiteri Mamaru, another chief, was baptized at the opening of the new Wesleyan Chapel at Waikouaiti on July 30, 1843, and two months later was appointed to act as a leader at Moeraki.

Merekihireka Hape, who later became a prominent chief, was baptized by Watkin on September 10, 1843, and was married by Creed in 1846. He was a useful and zealous teacher at Temuka and elsewhere, and subsequently became a lay reader in the Anglican Church at Waikouaiti.

One of the best known of the Maori chiefs was Tohiti Haereroa, who had been a great and relentless warrior in his day. Haereroa was a Maori of the best type. On one occasion he saved the life of a slave whom Karetai wished to kill and eat, by throwing his own mat over the shoulder of the captive. He had rather a good command of the English tongue and he was for a time in 1840 in the personal service of Mr. Watkin, assisting him mainly in perfecting the missionary's knowledge of the native language and in compiling his vocabulary. Haereroa, who was also known as ' Tommy Roundhead,' had shared in many a sanguinary battle, and he delighted to entertain and incidentally to shock Mr. Watkin with his graphic descriptions of these fights and their cannibal accompaniments. He professed conversion to the Christian faith, and on May 20, 1843, Mr. Watkin records that he had become anxious for Christian knowledge. Haereroa used to assist the whalers by notifying them of the proximity of whales by means of a beacon. One day he was visited in his ' look-out ' by some whalers. The spokesman said,

' Well, Tommy, have you seen any whales lately ? '

' Yes,' he answered, ' I saw one on Sunday.'

' Then why didn't you make a smoke ? ' they demanded, whereupon the native replied, ' Because it was the sacred day.'

By derisive laughter, and by ribald abuse, as well as by more cogent argument, they strove to shake his faith, but this proving unavailing, they left him, saying with the inflexion of disgust, ' Ugh, are you turned missionary, Tommy ? '

He died in the faith at Temuka about the year 1870. How rich and real had been the work of grace in their hearts was proved by the lives of Haereroa and many other men of chiefly rank.

The response of the leaders of Southern Maoridom to the appeal of the Christian evangel is further attested in a publication issued in 1873 entitled *A Compendium of Official Documents Relative to Native Affairs in the South Island*. In the second volume of that publication it is set forth that from the principal men of Maoridom five native Assessors or Magistrates were appointed in September 1864. All these men had been baptized by the Wesleyan missionaries between June 18, 1843, and June 29, 1845. Of the twenty-six principal men officially catalogued in the Maori aristocracy in the eight chief centres of native population, no fewer than nineteen had been baptized or married by the Wesleyan missionaries and two of the others had presented their children for baptism.

Owing to the Maori habit of using now one part, and now another, of their names, it is not always easy to identify them. Five names of noble lineage I do not recognize in the mission registers that are now in my custody, and one of these is Tohiti Haereroa, to whom reference has already been made. Chieftainship counting for what it did amongst the Maoris it was little wonder that most of the people of Southern Maoridom linked up with the Wesleyan Mission.

CHAPTER XVIII

TRANSFORMING MAORI CHARACTER

Heaven doth with us as we with torches do :
Not light them for ourselves ; for if our virtues
Did not go forth of us, 'twere all alike
As if we had them not. Spirits are not finely touched
But to fine issues.

—SHAKESPEARE.

JAMES WATKIN was never in a hurry for spiritual results. Realizing that he was building for eternity he cared more for qualities of character in his converts than for imposing statistics of success. For over two years he toiled with devoted zeal before he conducted the first public baptism, upon profession of faith, of one of his own Maori converts. This convert was named Mahaka. He was the first South Island Maori whom Watkin ever saw. He was one of the first whom the missionary taught to read and write and was the first to manifest any real religious concern.

Watkin had officiated at earlier Maori baptisms but they did not satisfy his heart-hunger for spiritual success springing out of his own work. On January 21, 1841, he had baptized Hoani Tokonui, a dying youth of twenty. This lad had, in accordance with Maori custom, been put in an outhouse to die, and his appearance at his baptism was very affecting. Immediately he was dead his friends, following native practice, trussed him up for burial in a sitting posture. A shallow grave was scooped among the sandhills and the remains were committed to Mother

174

Earth.   This was the first Christian burial of a native that ever took place in Southern New Zealand.

On January 27, 1841, Watkin had baptized Meri Kauri, of Bluff, on her marriage to James Palmer, a whaler who desired the missionary to sanctify their existing union. On January 9, 1842, he had baptized Hohepa Korehi, a convert of the Rev. Samuel Ironside, who had come from Port Underwood to act as a native teacher, and on December 4 of the same year he administered the rite to Meri Pikaurera, a dying child of nine summers.

But what made Watkin's heart sing when Mahaka was baptized on Christmas Day of 1842 was that the native really represented the first-fruits of his own toil.   Mahaka, who had undergone special preparation for three months in a class meeting, chose as his baptismal name that of his spiritual father and henceforth was known as Hemi Watekini Mahaka, or more familiarly as ' Jimmy Watkin.' This Maori namesake of the missionary had his religious vicissitudes but did useful service in many ways.   The day of his baptism Watkin regarded as the real natal day of the Christian Church in Otago.   It was certainly a day set in golden letters in the missionary's own calendar.

The increasing success of Watkin's work now necessitated a chapel of larger dimensions than the old ' whare karakia ' at the rear of the Mission House.   Arrangements were therefore made for a new place of worship.   This was in course of erection in May 1843.   In the following month there met at Waikouaiti an assembly of Ngai-Tahu tribes-men gathered from places as far apart as Cloudy Bay and Ruapuke.   So great was the influx of visitors that the service on June 19 was held in the frame of the new chapel.   On this occasion, amid a hush of reverence, Mr. Watkin baptized nineteen adult Maori men, two Maori women and one native child, and he records that the baptizing of hundreds in Tonga had never given him more pleasure than administering the rite to this small group of poor Maoris.

The new chapel was formally opened for public worship, though still in an unfinished state, on July 30, 1843. It was an interesting occasion. Outside the church, which stood on the ancient tribal assembly ground on Haute-kapakapa Hill, a ground that, through long generations, had witnessed many a gathering of the clan to debate the issues of war and peace, was the vision of a gaily moving throng of worshippers. Standing apart was a group of candidates for baptism receiving a few final instructions from the missionary. Their serious yet radiant faces— visible summaries of vital things invisible—proclaimed the transformations grace had wrought. The flush of the sun shone on their brown faces. The air stirred as with the breath of angels as the people entered the sanctuary. The rough building seemed lit with light celestial and a new glory gilded its shadows. Out of the black night of heathenism these Maoris had come to the dark and storm-swept plains of religious disillusionment, but with the coming of the missionary there stole down the obliterating darkness a grey dawn followed by the glory of a sunrise.

At this opening service five young men were received into church fellowship by baptism. They were Hoana Maka Wharepirau, of Waikouaiti, Anaru Tatairaki of Rakiura, and three from Moeraki, namely Hamiora Tahuanuku and the chiefs Rawiri Waiteri Te Mamaru and Matiaha Tiromorehu.

Although these converts had turned away from old vices they were not yet perfect. Heirs as they were to generations of heathen horrors, base desires still cried in them for satisfaction, and sparks of passion from quenched corruption's earlier fires were ready to leap again into flame. But though the drift of heredity still carried them, a new resistance had become manifest, and though evil still quivered in the nerves and throbbed in the blood the entail of sin had been broken. It lay beyond the power of the missionary to pour purer blood into their veins and to graft

TE MATENGA TAIAROA,
The Famous Fighting Chief of Otakou.

MR. JOHN JONES.

better tissues on their brains, but he had become to them a channel of the Divine grace that modifies, reverses and masters alike the influence of heredity, the power of environment and the thrall of habit.

Up till this time Mr. Watkin had baptized about fifty Maoris, only three of whom were children. Most of them could read and possessed some portion of the printed Scriptures, their knowledge of which was good and their applications of it apt. The year 1843 was one of ingathering after Watkin's patient seed-sowing, and by the close of the year he had baptized over two hundred converts and a gracious revival was in progress. On Christmas Eve of that year over two hundred persons attended morning service and more than fifty received baptism. At a Love Feast held in the afternoon many of the natives bore striking testimony to God's transforming grace. The preacher at the evening service was Hoani Weteri Korako, and at the Holy Communion which followed large numbers of Maoris took the solemn vow of allegiance to Jesus Christ. The Christmas of 1843 was one of joy in the heart of the missionary and in the life of many a dusky disciple of the missionary's Master.

On Boxing Day Mr. Watkin gave the natives a feast at which many Maori and European games were played. The native girls especially entered with zest into their pretty poi posture dances with twirling flax balls manipulated to the accompaniment of rhythmical movements of the body and the notes of lilting melodies.

Two months after Matiaha Tiramorehu was baptized he was appointed a leader and teacher at Moeraki and became one of Mr. Watkin's foremost helpers. He had studied in the Maori ' whare kura,' or house of higher learning, in which instruction was imparted in historical traditions, religious ritual and the higher ' mysteries ' that were known to the initiated. Matiaha possessed a wonderful store of occult lore and tribal traditions that had been passed on from generation to generation and was

M

without a rival in his knowledge of genealogical antiquities. He was devoted to the cause of the Mission and set an example to most of the Europeans in consistency of Christian conduct.

An instance of this was recorded by Mr. Watkin on January 20, 1844. A sub-Protector of the Maoris, who had been in the neighbourhood of Moeraki and was gathering materials for a book, asked Matiaha for information. This was freely given as far as time would allow, and on Saturday it was proposed by the sub-Protector that they should renew the theme next day.

' No,' was the firm answer of Matiaha.

' Why ? ' asked the visitor.

' Because it is the Sabbath,' responded the native.

' But I am leaving on Monday,' urged the pakeha.

' Never mind that,' was the crushing rejoinder. ' If the day is common to you, it is sacred to me.'

Matiaha did good service by his correspondence with Governor Eyre in 1849 to get a just allocation of reserves set apart for his tribe in the South Island. Mr. Walter Mantell, the Commissioner of Lands, in a report to the Colonial Secretary concerning Native Reserves, dated August 30, 1849, paid a high tribute to this ' Wesleyan teacher and principal man of the place,' from whom he stated he derived the greatest support and assistance.

Anaru Tatairaki, of Rakiura (Stewart Island), became a candidate for the office of native teacher shortly after his baptism. He was required to preach a trial sermon before a congregation that included the European missionary. Anaru was somewhat self-confident, and, like many another aspirant to the pulpit, thought preaching no very difficult task. He had read the third chapter of the Epistle of James upon which he purposed discoursing. Bent on making an impression he had marshalled a fine array of words. They sped like a flash from his mind to his glottis, which refused to lend itself to his purpose. His mouth opened and his lips moved but only a confused sound shot across the vastness of his vanished self-satisfaction. Mr. Watkin wrote the comment, ' Perhaps it has done Andrew good.' It certainly did, for he became an effective teacher, and after doing creditable work died in March 1845 at the early age of twenty-eight.

Another native teacher who was well versed in Maori lore was Horomona Pohio, who had been Watkin's principal helper on Ruapuke Island, but was at the period of the arrival of the Scottish settlers assisting the Rev. Charles Creed in mission activities between Waikouaiti and Dunedin. He used to tell of a traditional race of cave-dwelling ogres who possessed the power of flight and who sent out two-headed dogs to capture the first Maori migrants for their masters. This native had been taught to read and write by Watkin and he signed the register as a witness to the first Maori marriages performed by the missionary. In 1859 he became one of the native assessors for Otago and Southland and as late as 1864 was exercising the office of magistrate at Waitaki.

Rawiri Te Maire was another outstanding figure attached to the Wesleyan Mission. He became a constant companion to Watkin on his journeys by sea and land and a loyal lieutenant in ministerial service. Te Maire as a boy had lived at Lake Hawea, but had to flee with his people from Te Puohu, who, bent on exterminating the occupants of the South Island, had travelled overland from the west coast with a war party, leaving a trail of blood as he passed on to Tuturau, where he met his doom. Te Maire was married by Mr. Watkin on June 19, 1841, to Heikuna, who was later known as ' the Bo'sun.' This was one of the first four Maori marriages performed according to Christian usage in Otago, and all took place on the same date. It was at the instigation of Te Maire that the name of Hikororoa was changed to Mount Watkin. This native later joined the Anglican Church. He died in 1899 and was buried on the Mission Hill at Waikouaiti.

Another prominent chief who became a native teacher

and class leader was Hoani Weteri (John Wesley) Korako. He preached a creditable trial sermon on December 26, 1843. Tiare Weteri (Charles Wesley) Te Kahu, a chief well versed in Maori nomenclature, was a loyal friend of the missionaries and was often their companion in travel and service.

The most intellectual of all the Maoris at Waikouaiti in the whaling and mission days was one Maru, who was the Achilles amongst the tohungas or priests of the region. The character of this chief showed a rude Homeric grandeur. He eschewed witchcraft and had evidently emancipated himself from the trammels of the gross superstitions of his people and from the belief in malignant deities. He was a virtuous man of upright life and had never eaten human flesh or fallen into the low vices of the natives. For some years he kept aloof from the missionaries but was groping after a god of noble worth. In Io, the supreme head over all things in the Maori theologic system, he saw the shadow of One from Whom all things proceed.

When, on June 15, 1844, the day before Watkin left Waikouaiti for Wellington, he married Joseph Crocome, a surgeon, to Arapera Raureka, his Maori mate, Maru signed the register as a witness, together with Mrs. Watkin and the Rev. Charles Creed, a truly remarkable grouping of diverse personalities.

During the term of Mr. Creed, Maru began to attend the Wesleyan services. He would slip in at the back and sit in the corner remotest from the preacher. Maru told Mr. Creed that the natives of his tribe had been diabolically cannibal. One night as Creed was preaching on the words, ' Christ the power of God and the wisdom of God ' (1 Corinthians, chapter i. verse 24) he illustrated his theme by references to Maui, the incarnate god of the Maori, Maru shouted out, ' Koe-a, Koe-a, Koe-a ' (Yes! Yes!! Yes!!!).

As Mr. Creed proceeded to show how Jesus incarnated the power and the wisdom of God, the old tohunga, deeply moved, exclaimed, 'Kamou te korero' (Thy words are true). From that time the whole soul of the converted priest lived unto Christ. On May 30, 1847, he was baptized as Hohepa (Joseph) Entwisle Maru. He was a pattern to all and through his influence other chiefs were converted, gave up polygamy and similar practices and remained true to the 'Karakia,' or Christian worship.

It is worthy of note that within four years of commencing his work Mr. Watkin had trained and planted twenty-six native teachers in the settlements from Moeraki to Stewart Island. Despite the chiefly rank of a majority of them they had no special gifts of intellect or of speech. The missionary 'lads,' as the Maori agents were called, acted as village pastors and as itinerant preachers, held week-night services, led the class meetings and conducted schools. They had only a meagre training for their work and it is remarkable that so much was achieved so speedily with helpers so ill-equipped and so recently reclaimed from heathenism.

One has not captured the mystery and the glory of the springtime when he has plucked the dancing daffodil. Nor has one reached the confines of the ineffable when he has gathered the fruits of the Spirit in the children of Maoridom. These simple native converts—erstwhile cannibals some of them—knew nothing of any subtle philosophy of salvation. They could no more state the rationale of the Atonement than they could give the chemistry of colours or the mathematics of a sunrise. They only knew that they were free from the dread shadow of 'tapu' and from the tyranny of 'taipo'; that life was taking on tints of rarer beauty and that their daily lot was bright with a strange, rich radiance. That radiance was the reflection of the mysterious, all-satisfying shining of the face of the new-found Father. Their vision was still blurred, their knowledge of God still imperfect and the petals of the flower of a new life were only beginning to unfold. But they had heard whispers of love, faint at first, 'like an echo pulsing through a dream.' They had become conscious of ' murmurs and scents of the infinite sea ' and they had found fellowship with the mystic might that moulds the templed mountains ; that shapes the shining spheres and breathes in the fragrance of the forest. In that genial fellowship with the All-Father the old haunting horror of grim gods had melted like a wraith of mist.

Chapter XIX

NOBLE SERVICE ON A NARROW STAGE

' A commonplace life,' we say, and we sigh,
But why should we sigh as we say ?
The commonplace sun in the commonplace sky
Makes up the commonplace day.
The moon and the stars are commonplace things,
And the flower that blooms, and the bird that sings ;
But dark were the world and sad our lot
If the flowers failed, and the sun shone not.
And God who studies each separate soul
Out of commonplace lives makes the beautiful whole.

SOME of life's sweetest ministries walk forth from the
quiet places of earth, where men acquire strength and
fulness and beauty of character. Their lives are ordinary
and unromantic. Their outfit is meagre. They cause
no ripple on the sea of life. They have no greatness in
the eyes of men and only a scant chronicle on the pages
of history. The stamp of mediocrity is upon them. Yet
it is through mastery over mediocrity that the crowning
triumph of life is won. That triumph belongs, not to
those who have gained brilliant success, but to those
who, amid life's dreariest monotonies, have kept a great
soul in a small place. Such a triumph was achieved by
Johann Friedrich Heinrich Wohlers, whose noble service
on a narrow stage deserves the bestowal of the title ' the
apostle of Murihiku.'

The son of a peasant farmer Wohlers was born at
Mahlenstorf, Germany, on October 1, 1811. At this period
the territory was in the occupation of the conquering

armies of Napoleon. At the age of six the little lad went to live with his grandmother at Hoyerhagen, where he received instruction in the village school. Religious influences touched his early years but he felt little interest in the village church or its pastor.

Schooldays over he found employment on his uncle's farm at Hoyerhagen. The years sped, and at twenty-five we find him conscious of a lack of culture and ambitious for the higher learning that had been denied him. The sea of circumstance appeared to be bearing him towards the grey westward horizon. But, underlying the superficial movement of events, the Power that guides the destinies of the centuries was controlling his life with a fulness of purpose that outran human vision. Challenging circumstances and cosmic energies, like cog wheels working in opposite directions, were fitting into each other and producing an ordered result beyond the guessing of the buffeted young peasant.

His farm duties occasionally took Wohlers to the mill in the adjacent village of Vilsen, and here he found friends and fellowship in the household of the miller. The gateways of his life stood open. Through these portals any throbbing personality might enter to touch the springs of motion. The doors of destiny were entered by the medium of a missionary leaflet that Wohlers found one day on the miller's table. The leaflet contained a translation from the English of an appeal to British Methodists to undertake the evangelizing of Fiji. This appeal was written in 1836 by the Rev. James Watkin, then a missionary in the Friendly Islands. The reading of Watkin's words was the turning point of Wohler's life and awoke within him the desire to fulfil the vocation of a missionary. The following year the way opened for him to pursue studies in the Mission Institute of the Reformed North German Mission Union at Bremen. Here he remained until the end of 1842. He received his ordination, and the society directed him to proceed to New Zealand with three companions and to take equipment for establishing a mission farm. The party left Hamburg in the ship *St. Pauli* on December 26, 1842, and arrived at Nelson in the middle of June, 1843. A few days later tidings reached Nelson of the Wairau Massacre that had taken place on June 17. The story of that tragic encounter the present writer often heard from the lips of the Rev. Samuel Ironside, who was at the time in charge of the Wesleyan Mission at Cloudy Bay. The causes and consequences of that disaster justify a slight digression.

The trouble originated in a land dispute between Te Rauparaha and Colonel Wakefield of the New Zealand Company. The land in question was occupied by the Rangitane tribe, which had been conquered by the Ngatitoa Maoris under Te Rauparaha. Wakefield contended that the land had been sold to the New Zealand Company. This was denied by Te Rauparaha and his nephew Rangihaeata. The ownership of the land was also claimed by the chiefs resident at Wairau. One of these was Rawiri Kingi Puaha, a Wesleyan native teacher, who had been baptized by Ironside and married at Ngakuta on August 1, 1841. Captain Wakefield, a brother of the Colonel, approached Puaha with the offer of a small schooner and some goods if he would state that the disputed territory had been purchased by the Colonel. This, Puaha, with chiefly dignity, refused to do.

Despite protests Wakefield proceeded with the survey of the land. Te Rauparaha and his nephew now took a hand, and, coming with armed followers in their canoes, they prepared to destroy the camps of the surveyors. The hurried sequence of tragic events need not be related. The Rev. Samuel Ironside, who was well versed in Maori laws and customs, and who knew how critical the situation was, wrote a letter to Captain Wakefield. The letter was delivered on June 12. It stated that unless the situation was handled very diplomatically the result might be extremely serious. Had the letter been heeded the

massacre and all its dire results would have been averted.
Captain Wakefield, influenced by Ironside's letter, desired
to return to Nelson, but was overborne by Mr. Thompson,
a surveyor, and Mr. Richardson, the Crown Prosecutor.
The former was determined to give the natives a lesson
and, incidentally, to teach the Government how to deal
with savages; the latter stupidly regarded the whole
sorry business as 'only a lark.' Alas that they and a
score of others a few days later paid the penalty of their
folly with their lives.

When a clash seemed imminent the noble Wesleyan
chief, Puaha, with his Bible in his hand, exhorted both
pakeha and Maori to maintain the peace, but blunder
followed blunder and the climax was reached on June 17
when the survey party was slaughtered. Hearing that
his worst fears had been realized Ironside hastened in a
whale boat to Ocean Bay, and here he met Te Rauparaha
and Rangihaeata. The missionary asked permission to
go and bury the dead. Rangihaeata said it would be better
to leave them to the pigs but added that Ironside might
go if he liked and that he would find the bodies un-
mutilated. With a Maori crew and in the teeth of a gale
he crossed twelve miles of open sea and on arriving at
Tua Marina gave the bodies Christian burial. For his
heroism and his humane service he was held in high esteem,
but the massacre resulted in smashing his thriving Mission.

The tumult of excitement in Nelson in consequence of
the massacre of so many white men by the Maoris gave
Wohlers and his fellow-missionaries the first thrill of their
colonial life. Inquiring as to church conditions they found
that the Rev. John Aldred was in charge of the Wesleyan
cause at Nelson and that there was also a resident Anglican
minister. They also learned that the Maori people had,
for the most part, adopted Christian customs and that
native teachers were resident in their various settlements.
The almost Pentecostal success of the Wesleyan Mission
at Cloudy Bay impressed them. That success is further

attested by the registers kept by the Rev. Samuel Ironside.
These registers are now open before me as I write. They
show that on one day, August 7, 1842, the missionary
baptized as many as 177 converts and married thirty-nine
native couples according to the rites of the Christian
Church. These natives had their homes at Pisgah Vale,
D'Urville Island, Pelorus River and Tory Channel. A
week later (August 14) he baptized 142 more converts
and married thirty-one couples, most of them hailing from
Queen Charlotte Sound. From the inception of the
Mission in December 1840 to May 14, 1843, Ironside
baptized 680 adults and 168 children, and in the same
period married 188 couples. Then came the land dispute
and the massacre with all their shattering consequences.
A month after the tragedy Ironside baptized two natives
at Totara Nui and some time later an English child at
Ocean Bay. There the register ended and Ironside
proceeded to take up work at Wellington.

Always unwilling to interfere with the labours of others
Wohlers decided to work on the land in the Upper Moutere
Valley while awaiting a truly missionary sphere. Early
in 1844 he was offered by Frederick Tuckett, the surveyor,
an opportunity of a trip in the *Deborah*, a schooner of 121
tons burthen. Tuckett proposed going south in quest
of a site for a Scottish Free Church Settlement. Wohlers
accepted the offer, and while in Wellington called on the
Rev. Samuel Ironside. Ironside gave him a letter of
introduction to the Southern natives and introduced him
to the Rev. Charles Creed, who would also be travelling
by the *Deborah* in order to succeed Mr. Watkin at
Waikouaiti.

When the *Deborah* arrived at Port Cooper (Lyttelton)
on April 5 several natives boarded the schooner. These
included Tuhawaiki, the great chief whose authority
and influence extended from the far south to Banks
Peninsula, and Taiaroa, both of whom were clad in sailor
costumes. Wohlers handed Ironside's letter to Tuhawaiki,

who, however, could not read. He asked a native to decipher it for him and then assured Wohlers of a welcome to his domains.

Mr. Tuckett decided to spend a few days testing the suitability of Banks Peninsula for a settlement. The Wesleyan Mission had two native teachers named Taawao and Hohepa on the Peninsula. On the Sunday, Creed invited Wohlers to accompany him on a visit to a Maori village a few miles distant to conduct Divine service. A native gave directions for finding the place. As the two men climbed the hills a thick fog enveloped them. The sun became obscured and as they were without a compass they lost their way and at length found themselves at Lake Ellesmere instead of on the northern side of Banks Peninsula. Tired, hungry and foodless they searched for fuchsia berries and wild turnip and also managed to catch two small birds. Wohlers had a flint and steel and a small quantity of tinder, which was supplemented by a piece of Creed's shirt. With these they kindled a fire and cooked the birds and turnip leaves on which they regaled themselves. From Sunday until the following Wednesday they wandered over hills shaped by Nature's cataclysmic spasms, Creed bearing a burden of anxiety about his young wife and little child, who were on board the *Deborah*. At last they came in sight of Port Cooper, where their ship lay at anchor, but so difficult was the country that not until next morning could they reach the beach. A boat from the *Deborah* put off for the exhausted men, whose boots were worn out and whose clothes hung in rags about them.

Wohlers was advised by Tuckett to settle amongst the natives on the Peninsula but as the place was already under the care of the Wesleyan Mission he declined to intrude in a field that was then being adequately worked.

Continuing her journey southward on April 11 the *Deborah*, after a week of trying weather, reached Moeraki, where the Wesleyan Mission outpost was in charge of

resident native teachers. Proceeding on her way the
schooner reached Waikouaiti Bay on April 19, and when
the *Deborah* had cast anchor Mr. Watkin came on board,
shook hands with Creed, his successor, and exclaimed
half-jokingly : ' Welcome to purgatory, Brother Creed ! '

At Waikouaiti, Wohlers received the hospitality of the
Wesleyan mission house for the four days the *Deborah*
remained in the bay sharing a room with one of Watkin's
little sons. Watkin and Creed both encouraged Wohlers
to think favourably of settling at Ruapuke to exercise a
ministry amongst the Maoris of Murihiku, a sphere in which
Watkin had planted his teachers but to which he himself
could not give much personal service. Once again it
seemed as if the key was being turned by Watkin in
Wohler's door of destiny.

The pilot of the *Deborah* was Edward Palmer. While
at Waikouaiti, Palmer had, through the influence of Watkin,
professed conversion, and as the schooner sailed southward
he was commended to the pastoral care of Wohlers.
Arriving off Ruapuke Island they found a number of natives
assembled on the beach to hear whatever news the schooner
might bring. Wohlers stepped into a small boat in charge
of Palmer. As they got into shallow water natives waded
out to meet them. To these Palmer explained, in language
half English and half Maori, that he had, with the approval
of Mr. Watkin, brought a missionary who would remain
amongst them. The new arrival was carried ashore on
the back of a native. His scanty belongings, consisting
of a portmanteau, a gun, an axe, a saw, a sack of flour,
and a bag of salt were landed in the same fashion.

Despite the desire of Watkin the natives felt little
disposed to place themselves under the ministry of a man
who was a stranger to them and to their language. Some
of the Wesleyan teachers sent a boat to Waikouaiti to
lodge their protest against being disposed of without
their consent. Meanwhile Wohlers kept calmly on his
course, confident that Creed would not take sides against

him. He found Christian usages to be fairly general. Prayer meetings were held every night and morning. The Wesleyan and Anglican teachers persisted in maintaining their denominational distinctions and objected to Wohlers discharging sacred functions. Wohlers, therefore, in 1846, set himself to erect his own sanctuary and to serve the spiritual needs of the people so far as was possible without founding a Church of any particular denomination, or even establishing a permanent station for the North German Missionary Society.

Upon his arrival at Ruapuke Wohlers was at first quartered in the house of Tuhawaiki. It was a rough wooden cottage with a thatched roof. In front were two small windows and a door. There were two little bedrooms and a lean-to which served as kitchen and living room. As there were no chairs an upturned bucket served as a seat. Wohlers had a bed to himself but shared his room with a native. Some slept on the floor of the other bedroom but most on the earth floor of the kitchen. Later on he was offered the use of a house by Tione Topi Patuki, a chief next in rank to Tuhawaiki, and then in training for a Wesleyan native teacher. In the house in question Topi's first wife had died. It was therefore ' tapu,' or sacred, and as Wohlers must not enter the house where it stood, it was removed and rebuilt elsewhere. The place was fifteen feet long and nine feet wide. The walls were only four feet high and the door somewhat less. The walls and roof were thatched with reeds and grass. The chief compensation was that the hut was set amidst beautiful surroundings and some distance from the disgusting stench and filth of the whares in the native village.

Several years passed in patient, unremitting toil throughout the region of Foveaux Straits. It was toil marked by alternations of discouragement and success. For four years no financial support had come from the Missionary Society in Germany. The chief stimulus of Wohler's life was furnished by cheery letters constantly coming

from Creed at Waikouaiti. The lonely man confessed
that labour and ill-nourishment had weakened his body,
affected his mental powers and induced a confused
melancholy. Mr. Creed wrote urging him to come for a
visit to Waikouaiti. Accordingly at the end of 1847 he
set out in an open boat with a Maori crew and fairly
revelled in the family life of the Wesleyan mission house.
Creed radiated good cheer and took him wherever the
company might afford a mental tonic, including a wedding
which Wohlers attested in the register by signing as a
witness. For two months he shared the life of the mission
house at Waikouaiti, over which Mrs. Creed presided
with gracious charm. Greatly refreshed he returned to
his post, but here all was so desolate that melancholy
again nearly overcame him. He felt himself deserted by
his home society. At the end of 1848 another agent
arrived from Germany, but brought no money for the
maintenance of the work. Instead a letter came directing
him to repair to Nelson to ordain a missionary there.

Once again he set out from Ruapuke in an open Maori
boat. At Port Chalmers he put his luggage on a vessel
bound for Wellington and himself went overland to visit
the Creeds at Waikouaiti. Their home drew him like a
magnet. He was now thirty-eight years old. His clothes
were worn, his body ill-nourished, his spirit restless and
unhappy. With swift intuition Mrs. Creed had long ago
diagnosed his malady and now determined upon a cure.
She was confident that the exiled bachelor would, with
wifely care and fellowship, become a new man and find
life a joyous adventure. She wrote out her diagnosis
of the case and also her prescription in the form of a letter
of introduction and sent it by the hand of Wohlers himself
to a friend in Wellington who had not long been widowed.
This was Mrs. Elise Palmer, a gracious lady who had a
good knowledge of the Maori people and of their language.

Wohlers executed his commission at Nelson and returned
to Wellington, where the Rev. James Watkin was super-

intendent of the Wesleyan circuit, and once more Wohlers became his guest. As the host and his friend sat by the fire, comfortably smoking their pipes, Watkin asked Wohlers what had led him to become a missionary. The visitor told how, before he knew anything concerning missions, a leaflet had come into his hands in the house of a miller in the German parish of Vilsen. The first article he read was about the heathen in Fiji, and it had so impressed him, that still, after a dozen years, he could repeat the contents. Both men were stirred by deep emotion as they discovered that the article was the appeal that Watkin himself had written in 1836.

Having thus, unconsciously and by strange providences been largely instrumental in Wohler's choice of a vocation, and in his choice of a sphere of labour, Watkin's hand was once again near the latch on his friend's door of destiny. This third opening of that door was going to let Wohlers out of his cage and free him from the fettering influences and the trivial commonplaces that were operating to cramp and belittle his life. God, the universe, man, life, were about to assume bigger proportions. His approaching marriage by Watkin to a bride yet unknown, unmet and unwon, was going to widen his intellectual horizons and to lead him henceforth to claim infinity for workshop and playroom.

Mrs. Creed's letter of introduction reposed in the pocket of Wohlers. Seeking directions from Watkin he lost little time in effecting a delivery of the missive. He was immensely impressed with the lady and surprised himself with the fervour of his wooing, although he declared that the only dowry he could offer was a sphere of operations. Pressing his proposal the lady objected mainly on the grounds that they knew so little of each other and that the suggestion had originated with others and had not spontaneously sprung from their own inclinations. Wohlers persisted that marriages were made in heaven, and that Mrs. Creed was as good as an angel of heaven,

REV. J. F. H. WOHLERS.

whereupon the lady consented and in a few days James Watkin officiated at their marriage.

Wohlers and his bride took passages in the barque *Cornwall*, bound for Dunedin, where they landed on September 23, 1848, and as no vessel was sailing for Ruapuke they went by a Maori boat to spend their honeymoon with the Creeds at Waikouaiti. Mrs. Creed was delighted with the success of her match-making. The newly married couple landed at their island home on December 1, 1848, and here the gracious influence of Mrs. Wohlers operated to transform life on Ruapuke, where she ruled like a queen. In 1850 they had the misfortune to lose their home by fire. Everything was burnt, including his books and papers. Wohlers conducted worship, taught school, acted as registrar of births, marriages and deaths, cultivated his garden and carried out pastoral work. In every good work his wife shared with devoted zeal. His mission staff was reinforced by the arrival of a helper who settled on Stewart Island, and by several artizans from Germany. Wohlers continued his beneficent work for Murihiku Maoridom until death overtook him at Stewart Island, on May 7, 1885. He was survived by his noble wife and devoted daughter, to whom he bequeathed the fragrant memory of a simple, self-forgetting life of service. The minds of the Maoris as he found them were in the twilight. Old lamps were flickering and new had just been lit.

In that prehistoric creature, the archeopteryx, biologists declare that the scales of the reptile were evolving into the feathers of the bird, and there was latent within an energy that transformed the repulsive ugliness of the creature of the slime into the bewitching beauty of a bird of paradise. Assisted by their wives, Watkin and Creed in their larger sphere, and Wohlers on his narrower stage, saw the hidden potentialities in the nature of the Maoris and their capacity to respond to higher things than they yet had dreamed. So they planted deep in the hearts of the natives a new ideal. That ideal summoned into activity their unguessed inner powers and called to its aid and to its testing the resources of the Divine Renewer of men. They led many a Maori from the gloom into the glory, and the track they travelled became strewn with the wreckage of discarded deities and hateful heathen practices.

Chapter XX

PREPARING FOR A NEW COLONIZATION

Grant us the will to fashion as we feel,
  Grant us the strength to labour as we know,
Grant us the purpose, ribbed and edged with steel
    To strike the blow.

Knowledge we ask not—knowledge Thou hast lent,
  But Lord, the will—there lies our bitter need.
Give us to build above the deep intent
    The deed, the deed.
                                —John Drinkwater.

Mr. E. G. Wakefield, in his *View of the Art of Colonization*, published in 1849, said that the Wesleyan Methodist Church must be awarded first rank in point of efficiency as a colonizing Church. He wrote : ' It goes before settlement. It penetrates into settlements where there is no religion at all and gathers into its fold many of those whom the other Churches utterly neglect.'

Though the odious comparison may justly be rejected the tribute well may stand. Indeed it was echoed over fifty years later by Theodore Roosevelt, who declared that the pioneer preachers of a militant Methodism were often ' the first harbingers of civilization ' in the world's dark places as, with fiery zeal, they carried on their ' grim struggle against the forbidding forces of wild nature and of wilder men.'

In the early days of the great Evangelical Revival of the eighteenth century John Wesley overleaped all geographical bounds and all social and racial barriers when he made that great affirmation ' I look upon all the world as my parish.' His limitless vision of the mission of Methodism was again dramatically demonstrated in 1772, when on sending a pioneer preacher across the Atlantic he wrote, ' I let you loose on the great continent of America. Publish your message in the open face of the sun.' Imbued with the spirit of their founder the Methodists had, by the first quarter of the nineteenth century, crossed every ocean and established missionary centres under almost every sky. They did not aim at being a colonizing Church in the sense of establishing sectarian settlements or class communities. They simply sought to obey the injunction of Wesley to go, not merely to those who needed them, but to those who needed them most. Under the impulse of that motive they had come to New Zealand. Here they found that one of the greatest obstacles to their work was created by white men, who had cunningly filched from the natives the best of their lands. Their harbours were appropriated, their forests cleared, familiar haunts and vantage grounds were fenced off, the movements of the Maoris were restrained and disabilities were imposed upon them. Typical of many transactions was one in which John Jones claimed to have bought in 1839 a block of land from the mouth of the Waikouaiti River to Matainaka Heads and for a distance of ten miles inland for a tierce of tobacco and ten dozen cotton shirts. Similar trafficking had been going on all over the country. It is little wonder that when the Maoris saw the magnitude of the white invasion and the consequences to their old way of life their hearts were hot with resentment and that a sowing of fraud produced a reaping in bloodshed.

It is worthy of note that the Standing Regulations of the Wesleyan Methodist Missionary Society strictly forbade the missionaries acquiring property either in stock or in land at their mission stations. In a letter to Earl Grey in about the year 1847 it is stated that no Wesleyan missionary in New Zealand was allowed to hold, nor did in fact hold any land for his own private use, and that in the course of nearly thirty years only one of the missionaries had ever broken the regulation by purchasing land and engaging in commerce, and that he had been dismissed from the service of the society.

Dr. Lang in his book, *New Zealand in 1839*, stated that this refusal of the Wesleyan missionaries to trade in native land accounted for ' the greater success of the Wesleyan Mission as compared with the Church Mission.' That judgement finds confirmation in the voluminous report presented to the House of Commons in 1840, in which it is stated that in consequence of the Methodist missionaries, unlike others, refraining from trading in land, they commanded universal respect from the natives, whose welfare they zealously sought to promote.

High praise was given to the Revs. James Watkin and Charles Creed for their exertions in promoting the welfare of the natives in the South, in Volume I, part 2, page 20, of *A Compendium of Official Documents relative to Native Affairs in the South Island*, that was published in 1873.

In the same volume, on page 218, dealing with the subject of the Southern Native Reserves, a letter written by Mr. Walter Mantell, the surveyor, to the Honourable the Chief Secretary, on January 30, 1849, is quoted, in which a tribute is paid to the great support and assistance given him by the Wesleyan native teachers. Mr. Mantell adds that at Waikouaiti he asked the Rev. Charles Creed whether he would prefer the Mission Station which was close to the Maori pa to be included in, or left out of the Native Reserve, and that Mr. Creed had begged him, if possible, to include it in the Reserve, and that this was done. A similar case is recorded by Sir Walter Buller in a report dated March 1862, in which he states that for services rendered by the Wesleyans an area of four and a half acres at Kaiapoi was allocated as a ' Wesleyan Church Endowment,' but that the Church did not accept it, and the land still remained in the possession of the natives. Small areas of land in the North Island, barely sufficient for mission purposes only, were acquired by the Wesleyan Society.

For over a quarter of a century following upon the coming of Samuel Marsden in 1814, the Church of England, the Wesleyan Methodists and the Roman Catholics alone were carrying on well organized missionary enterprises amongst the Maoris and they still retain this pre-eminence. It was not until 1840 that the first Presbyterian congregation was formed in New Zealand. This was at Port Nicholson. Subsequently, the Rev. J. Duncan took up work for the Presbyterians in the Manawatu district, but at too late a period to have much influence upon the Maoris as a race. From the three historic missionary Churches many natives have been detached by the Ratana and the Ringatu movements as well as by the Mormons.

For some time the New Zealand Company had been looking to Otago as a possible region for founding a colony. In October 1842 one of its surveyors, Captain William Mein Smith, spent five days in the Otago district. He made a perfunctory sort of inspection and gathered unfavourable impressions. Early in the year 1843 the Company suggested a project for establishing a Scottish Presbyterian Settlement in New Zealand, but towards the end of that year differences developed with the British Government of a nature sufficiently serious to lead to a temporary suspension of the colonizing activities of the Company.

In May 1845 a number of members of the Free Church of Scotland formed themselves into a Lay Association for promoting a Scottish Settlement in New Zealand, but adverse political developments, lack of financial support, and the apprehension engendered by receipt of tidings of the Wairau Massacre and of Maori troubles in the North Island all conspired to delay fulfilment of their purpose.

Even the site for the future settlement remained undetermined, though it was anticipated that it might be
located at Port Cooper (Lyttelton).

Mindful of the colonizing project and desiring to
familiarize himself with local conditions, Sir George Grey,
the new Governor of New Zealand, paid a visit to Otago
early in 1844. He reached Waikouaiti on February 21
and was greatly impressed with the natives who were
paraded before him by Mr. Watkin. This visit began a
friendship that endured for long years between the
Governor and the missionary. Mr. Watkin recorded in
his diary that the Governor appeared to be a fast friend
of the missionaries and had promised to be a father to
the natives. That assurance the Governor renewed when,
on a subsequent visit, he was welcomed to Dunedin by
the Rev. Charles Creed in January 1848.

On March 31, 1844, Mr. Frederick Tuckett, a surveyor,
who had been appointed by Colonel Wakefield, of the
New Zealand Company, to choose a site for the projected
Scottish Settlement, left Nelson in the ship *Deborah*, of
121 tons, commanded by Captain Wing. The story of
his quest and of the choice of Otago for the ' New Edinburgh ' Settlement has been told so often that it needs
no extended reference here. The boat carrying the
surveyor and his party also brought the Rev. Charles Creed
to succeed Mr. Watkin in his missionary charge at
Waikouaiti. Mr. Watkin was to transfer to Wellington
on the return trip of the *Deborah* with the exploring party.

For nine weeks Watkin and Creed were together at
Waikouaiti. They followed with attention the search
for a site and were greatly interested in the subsequent
negotiations for the purchase of the Otago Block from
the native people.

On April 22, 1844, Mr. Watkin, after recording the
arrival of the *Deborah* at Waikouaiti, wrote that there was
some prospect of the New Edinburgh Settlement being
founded in that quarter. On June 4 he wrote: ' The

new settlement is to be in this neighbourhood, a thing which will contribute something to the comfort, and, as usual, something to the hindrance of the missionary.' He added, ' I expect this is the best choice yet made by the colonists.'

The negotiations for the purchase of the Otago Block took place at Koputai, now known as Port Chalmers. Some 150 natives interested in the transaction assembled from various parts of Otago. The eighteen canoes by which many had travelled, were drawn up on the beach. The *Deborah* lay quietly at anchor a short distance from the shore. The natives were a picturesque company, some being decked with albatross down and having feathers stuck through their nostrils. Many a clamorous discussion about the price of the land was conducted with Mr. Tuckett. The natives, having been Christianized by the agents of the Wesleyan Methodist Mission, assembled twice a day for worship and to seek the blessing of God upon their negotiations.

An agreement was ultimately reached, and on June 20, 1844, the Memorandum of Sale was signed by the three principal chiefs, Tuhawaiki, Karetai and Taiaroa. The completion of the sale was effected on July 31, 1844, when the Deed was signed by the three chiefs already mentioned and by twenty-two others of the Ngai-Tahu tribe. The purchase price was not, as in so many instances, paid in tobacco, tomahawks and blankets, but in bank notes, gold and silver distributed by Colonel Wakefield. The price paid for the entire block of 400,000 acres was £2,400, or less than three half-pence an acre.

The late Rev. Alexander Whyte, of Port Chalmers, stated that from the date of this purchase ' Otago has been consecrated ground.' As a matter of fact that Southern soil had been sanctified more than four years earlier when James Watkin opened his commission in the then un-evangelized area and began a work, the success of which was attested by the spirit in which his converts bore themselves throughout the protracted negotiations for the alienation of treasured tribal territories.

When Watkin sailed from Waikouaiti for Wellington on June 26, 1844, he left 227 Church members whom he had won from heathenism, and more than twenty-six native preachers and class leaders in the various Maori villages in Otago and Southland. He had baptized 268 persons, including some children, and had married thirty-nine couples, including two on the day of his departure. These last were the marriages of Europeans who had, until now, refused to marry their Maori concubines.

The mere statement of facts and of figures conveys some idea of the progress, position and prospects of the work of the pioneer preacher, but neither forms of speech nor the terms of arithmetic can express the spiritual realities of which they treat. Only a high voltage of sympathetic understanding can invest the record with palpitating vitality, and only a true imagination can transmute bare figures and bald facts into a fairer currency, the minted coins of which consist of transformed conditions and transfigured lives stamped with the image and superscription of a thorn-crowned King. But such was Watkin's record for four years of foundational work, work that Charles Creed continued to consolidate and extend for a further quadrennium before the arrival of the Scottish emigrants.

When the ship *John Wickliffe* reached Otago on March 23, 1848, and the *Philip Laing* on April 15 of the same year the first parties of Scottish settlers found solid moral foundations whereon to build. From wild and warring elements the pioneer Methodist missionaries had created a community having a corporate life and a Christian conscience. The rich life of the entire region has its roots, not only in Scottish soil, but largely in the work of Watkin and of Creed. To tell the story of the Province only from the establishment of the Free Church Settlement is to exhibit a flower without a root or a statue without a pedestal.

CHAPTER XXI

CHARLES CREED AND THE SCOTTISH SETTLEMENT

O my love, Dunedin town, the only, the abiding !
Sister of the mountain mist, and never to be holden
With the weary sophistries that dimmer eyes embolden—
O the dark Dunedin town, shot with green and golden !

Sleep you well, Dunedin town, though loud the lulling lyre is ;
Lady of the stars terrene, where quick the human fire is ;
Lady of the Maori pines, the turrets and the eyries.

JESSIE MACKAY.

THE Wairau Massacre of 1843, which shattered the Wesleyan Methodist Mission at Cloudy Bay, resulted also in breaking up the preaching squads of native teachers that had, under the Rev. Samuel Ironside, constantly visited all the Maori settlements from Port Underwood southward to the Waitaki River. The work of the Maori pastors who had been quartered in some of the native villages also languished when the only oversight exercised was such as could be given by Mr. Ironside from Wellington and by the Rev. John Aldred from Nelson.

With the coming of the Rev. Charles Creed to Waikouaiti the boundaries of his district, that until now had been from Foveaux Straits to the Waitaki River, were extended northward as far as the Kaikoura Mountains—a stretch of territory over four hundred miles long. A charge of such far-stretching distances, involving the pastoral oversight of the Maoris and white settlers throughout the region, called for a man of strong physique and of indomitable will.

Mr. Creed was a native of Somersetshire. He was

endowed with more than ordinary physical strength and possessed the determination characteristic of his county. Born in 1812 he entered the ministry in 1837, and when he came to Waikouaiti was only thirty-two years of age. He was one of a band of six distinguished ministers who left Gravesend on September 20, 1838, in the ship *James*, of 350 tons burthen, to reinforce the Wesleyan mission staff in the South Seas. Besides Mr. Creed the party included the Revs. John Waterhouse, John Egglestone, John H. Bumby, John Warren and Samuel Ironside. Upon arrival at Hobart Town the missionary party was entertained at Government House by Sir John Franklin, who later won fame as an Arctic explorer. Mr. Waterhouse and Mr. Egglestone disembarked at Hobart Town. The other members of the party reached Hokianga on March 19, 1839.

After a brief term at Hokianga and the Kaipara Mr. Creed was sent to Taranaki on board the missionary ship *Triton* and landed at Ngamotu on January 14, 1841. He was the first resident missionary amongst the Taranaki Maoris and his wife was the first European female to settle there. Mr. Creed was on the beach at New Plymouth in March 1841 to meet the men of Cornwall and of Devon who founded that settlement. The appointment of Mr. Creed to Taranaki was to meet the needs of the Maoris who, at that period, were returning from Cook Strait to their ancestral homes, and also of the returning exiles who were being emancipated from slavery in the Waikato. Of such importance was his appointment regarded by the Maoris that a young chief of Kai Iwi, one Reihana Toko, escorted him all along the coast during the first year of his work.

For over three years Mr. Creed worked in Taranaki and in 1844 was transferred to Otakou, a name that was officially changed to Otago on December 26, 1848. To his new charge Mr. Creed brought a supply of Testaments, hymn books and service books in the soft and euphonious

Waikato dialect. Having exceptional linguistic accomplishments he was a master of fluent and graceful speech, and by his wonderful felicity in the use of idiomatic Maori he gained a ready access to the native mind.

Charles Creed was a tireless traveller. By canoe, whaleboat or other available craft he ranged the rugged coast-line of his extensive charge. He also undertook long journeys on foot, both alone and accompanied by native companions. He was a good horseman and he and his steed ' Pompey ' were familiar figures in the 'forties. ' Pompey ' had the reputation of being something of an outlaw. When most needed he had a habit of disappearing and hiding amongst the reeds and undergrowth at Waikouaiti. Mr. Thomas Ferens, who for a time assisted Mr. Creed in school work and in preaching, recorded his firm conviction that the rebellious spirit of ' Pompey ' was due to 'some opposition of Satan' to the work of the mission.

A typical journey undertaken by Mr. Creed may be described. Accompanied by Rawiri te Maire, Wiremu Patene, and Hohepa Maru, he set out from Waikouaiti Bay on September 22, 1845, in a small schooner bound for Banks Peninsula. For four days in the face of a furious storm they beat up the coastline and at length cast anchor in the spacious harbour at Akaroa. Here they visited the European settlers, held services in the native villages, baptized prepared converts, and celebrated a number of marriages. Leaving Akaroa on October 5, 1845, they tramped over the hills to Port Levy, where about a dozen Europeans and some three hundred Maoris were settled. Mr. Creed conducted public worship, married three Europeans to native women and also united nine Maori couples according to Christian usages. Services were held at every native settlement on Banks Peninsula. Pigeon Bay, Rapaki and Port Cooper were visited and contact was established with several Europeans who had settled at the place last named.

Still on foot Mr. Creed and his three native helpers skirted the site of the future city of Christchurch and passed on to visit the Maori kaingas in the vicinity of Lake Ellesmere. After traversing the Canterbury Plains and fording many of its rivers, Mr. Creed recorded his conviction that ultimately this vast expanse would be made available for very extensive sheep and cattle runs. Turning their faces southward the itinerants called at all the native settlements along the route. They visited the old Te-wai-ate-ruati pa near Temuka, and in turn held services and conducted baptisms and marriages at Timaru, Makihikihi, Waitaki, Moeraki and other Maori villages nearer to Waikouaiti. After an absence of fifty-one days, on forty-seven of which they had travelled almost continuously on foot, they reached home on November 12.

Four weeks later, namely on December 10, 1845, Mr. Creed crossed over the Port Chalmers hills and held service at a small kainga called Tawhiroko, which was probably situated at Tayler's Bay. From here he passed on to Koputai, ministering to Maori and pakeha and then on to Otepoti. This was the first of many visits that Mr. Creed made to the site of the future city of Dunedin. When he came the hillsides were heavily timbered with tarata, mapau and other trees. Wild pigs were plentiful in the bush and pigeons and kaka birds abounded. The only white settlers in the locality were two runaway sailors who lived in a whare beside the sparkling Kaituna rivulet that flowed through the dense growths of fern, flax, toi toi and manuka and then ran into the sea among the rocks where the Dunedin Stock Exchange now stands. At this spot, in a little cove, the natives moored their canoes, and near by, in the vicinity of the present Cargill Monument, waves lapped a pebbly beach that was a favourite resort for the Maoris of the Otepoti pa.

Over the area now occupied by the city and suburbs of Dunedin a number of native settlements were scattered. The largest hapu lived at the Otepoti kainga. This embraced an area that is now enclosed roughly by Rattray, Maclaggan and Maitland Streets, and along Manor Place towards Market Street. For all practical purposes Otepoti may be regarded as the Maori name for the site of Dunedin. Indeed it is the name that was so used in 1854 on the receipts given by the natives when the final payments were made to them on account of the purchase of the Southland Block.

Charles Creed was the first preacher of any Church to conduct religious worship and to institute regular preaching services on the site of the future city. Not until February 23, 1846, did Mr. C. H. Kettle, a civil engineer, arrive from England to start the survey of the new town. A close friendship sprang up between the missionary and the chief surveyor and on his subsequent visits to Dunedin, Mr. Creed was invariably the guest of Mr. Kettle. Mr. Creed saw the birth and watched the growth of the infant capital of the Province of Otago, and during his visits to the natives as well as to the few Europeans who, by the end of 1847 occupied the houses that dotted the foreshore, he watched the preparations for the coming of the Scottish Free Church Settlement. He saw the building of the first barracks for the accommodation of the married emigrants who were coming by the ship *John Wickliffe*. A modest structure it was, made of rough uprights intersected with rustic branches and interlaced with long grass. The roof was thatched and there was no fireplace.

The first baptism of a European at Dunedin was conducted by Mr. Creed on October 29, 1846, the subject of this rite being Patric, the infant son of Mr. Robert Park, a civil engineer. This child had been born at Akaroa on August 2, 1846. The first birth of a white child at Dunedin took place on December 10, 1846, and this child— John Anderson—was baptized by Mr. Creed on April 11, 1847. On the same day he also baptized the first white girl ever born in Dunedin. This was Elizabeth Kettle, the daughter of the chief surveyor. The little maid was born on March 3, 1847. She subsequently became the wife of Mr. James Macassey, a distinguished solicitor. On March 10, 1847, Mr. Creed baptized Catherine, the infant daughter of Donald and Mary Ross. All these baptisms took place long before the advent of the Presbyterian pilgrims.

The ship *John Wickliffe*, with the first party of Scottish settlers, arrived on March 23, 1848. The Rev. Thomas Dickson Nicholson, who had come as a passenger and was proceeding northward, preached in the Immigration Barracks in Dunedin on the morning of April 9, 1848, and in the afternoon he preached amongst the baggage and stores that had been landed from the ship. The following day Mr. Creed was in Dunedin, having ridden, over from Waikouaiti in pursuit of his customary tasks. On Thursday, April 13, he conducted Divine worship in the Barracks.

The *Philip Laing*, bearing the Rev. Thomas Burns and the second draft of Scottish settlers arrived on Saturday, April 15, 1848. All were cordially welcomed by Mr. Creed, who undertook to make full arrangements for Mr. Burns to preach at the Barracks on the morning of Sunday, April 16. Mr. Creed attended this service and himself preached in the Barracks at 6.30 on the evening of the same day. Mr. Burns, writing to the Rev. John Sym of Edinburgh, on April 23, 1848, described Mr. Creed as ' an excellent, devoted man ' and expressed the hope that they would be able to strengthen each other's hands.

On Tuesday, April 18, Mr. Creed returned to Waikouaiti but he put the Dunedin Maoris of his flock under the temporary supervision of Mr. Thomas Ferens, a devoted Durham Methodist, who had arrived in the *John Wickliffe*, and who, with Mr. Henry Monson, a fellow-emigrant and loyal Wesleyan, did noble service for long years for every cause of truth and righteousness, and the record of whose work would require a very lengthy chronicle. Mr. Creed continued his ministrations alike to Maori and pakeha, while his native helpers maintained their regular visits to all the Maori settlements in which resident teachers had not been placed by the Rev. James Watkin and himself during the eight years in which the Wesleyan Methodist Mission had been carrying on its spiritual and educational work, and also dispensing medicine free of charge to brown men and to white.

A growing number of the white settlers at Dunedin, including many Anglicans, desired to share in the ministrations of Mr. Creed, who arranged for Divine worship to be conducted at the Gaol, the only suitable place available, every Sunday morning. John Wesley had enjoined his followers to use, in their Sunday morning services, his own abridgement of the order of worship as found in the Anglican ' Book of Common Prayer.' That custom was followed by all European congregations of Wesleyans throughout New Zealand in the early days. The practice extended also to the Maori congregations. From the Wesleyan printing press at Mangungu various publications were issued including one entitled ' The Prayers of the Church of England, commonly called The Wesleyan Prayer Book, adapted to the Wesleyan Service.' The stateliness and rhythm of the Liturgy made a strong appeal to Maori taste, and its sentences, fixed in their memory, became almost proverbial.

On the morning of Sunday, January 28, 1849, a large number of Anglicans were present at Mr. Creed's service. In accordance with time-honoured custom he used Wesley's abridgement of the Church of England order of morning worship. Finding that the Wesleyan service differed so little from their own traditional forms, many Anglicans resolved to throw in their lot with the Wesleyans until such time as their own Church took up work amongst them. On February 7 they inserted an advertisement in the *Otago Daily News*, a paper then published in Dunedin, informing the friends of the Established Church of Mr. Creed's services. The editor of the journal also commended

REV. CHARLES CREED.

the services to those who had all their life been attached
to Anglican forms of worship. The services met with
the loyal support of many who were not embraced in the
Presbyterian fold.

The *Otago Daily News* loosely referred to Mr. Creed's
services as Church of England services, and Dr. Hocken
following this cue erroneously described them as ' Episco-
palian services.' They were misled by confusing John
Wesley's revised and abridged version of the Book of
Common Prayer with the Church of England book itself.
It is not surprising, therefore, to find a modern writer,
like the late Rev. E. J. Neale, assuming that Mr. Creed
had, in some way, received authority to officiate at Church
of England services in Dunedin. Mr. Creed's salary was
independent of any support given on his station, and the
strict discipline of the Missionary Society, whose servant
he was, would not admit of him undertaking any official
position with another denomination. The Dunedin residents of 1849 regarded the services of Mr. Creed as simply
Wesleyan services. Mr. F. L. Mieville, quoting from his
Journal for the period under review, states that Mr. Creed,
who was always willing to help other denominations,
preached by special request of the Church of England
members, and that, as there was then no Anglican minister,
they were ' only too thankful to have the gospel preached
by this good Wesleyan minister.' Not even by Captain
Cargill and the Rev. Thomas Burns were the services of
Mr. Creed regarded other than as Wesleyan services.

The first Anglican minister to reside in Dunedin was
the Rev. J. A. Fenton, who came from the Canterbury
Settlement by appointment of Bishop Selwyn on January 1,
1852. In a sketch of the founding and progress of the
Anglican Church in Otago Mr. Fenton states that in
1851 the Church of England had ' no clergyman, no
building, no land and no money,' and he adds that some
of the Anglicans asked the Wesleyan missionary at
Waikouaiti to perform marriages and baptisms for them.

Mr. A. R. C. Strode, the resident magistrate, a son of Sir Edward Cheetham Strode, and the principal Anglican layman then in Dunedin, was married by Mr. Creed on March 14, 1851. Dr. Hocken records that Mr. Creed 'unswervingly continued his ministrations,' and it is gratifying to find that on March 10, 1852, the newly-formed committee of the Church of England cordially thanked Mr. Creed for his visits to Dunedin and for the performance of the services of the Church during the period prior to the coming of the Rev. J. A. Fenton. The committee further offered its sympathy to Mr. Creed because of the manner in which he had been attacked by Captain Cargill for so doing.

Through all the years of his planning for the Settlement the Rev. Thomas Burns kept his heart set upon establishing a sectarian colony. The attempt to make Otago a Presbyterian preserve was foredoomed to failure. Disappointed though he was at the breakdown of his cherished purposes, Dr. Burns writing to his brother as late as 1862, said that he still believed pronouncedly that class settlement was the only Christian mode of colonization. Many incidents reveal how that belief held him in its grip.

We have already seen that before the arrival of the Rev. Thomas Burns, Mr. Creed had baptized a number of European children at Dunedin, including a daughter of Mr. Donald Ross. On January 20, 1849, he baptized another child of Mr. Ross and also an infant daughter of Mr. William Alfred Moseley. Mr. Burns recorded in his diary on January 28 that without any communication from him Mr. Creed had baptized these children. What 'communication' the pioneer needed from the newcomer it is just as difficult to discover as it is to understand why, on March 18, 1849, Mr. Burns, from his pulpit, described the Scottish settlers as ' the depositaries of the Gospel ordinances and the means of grace at the remotest ends of the earth, where they were not known before.' As a matter of fact the Gospel ordinances and the means

of grace had been introduced nine years previously by
Wesleyans, and the region had also been slightly touched
by Bishop Pompallier, entered by Anglican native
teachers, visited by Bishop Selwyn and worked in one
area by a German missionary.

Dr. Merrington, the biographer of Dr. Burns, somewhat
severely says that the prejudices of Captain Cargill, the
agent for the Scottish Settlement, ran through narrower
channels than those of Burns, ' finding their way through
ruts of sectarianism and provincialism which wore deeply
into the surface of common life.' The agent bitterly
resented both the ministrations and the influence of the
Wesleyan missionary in Dunedin. On March 15, 1849,
he wrote to Mr. Creed accusing him of ' deserting his own
charge and intruding upon that of another.' He also
said that Mr. John Jones, who alleged that he had given
generous financial support to the mission, was deeply
aggrieved by Mr. Creed's frequent and long absences
from his proper charge at Waikouaiti.

This letter was not received by Mr. Creed until April 6.
He acknowledged it next day, protesting against the
intolerance of Captain Cargill and stating that as the letter
contained statements and principles of importance to
the general community he proposed to lay it before the
public with such information as was deemed requisite
to vindicate the Mission with which he had the privilege
to be connected.

The correspondence was published in the *Otago Daily
News* of May 2, 1849. Mr. Creed dealt trenchantly with
the criticisms of Captain Cargill, rebuked him for interfering with the duties of a Wesleyan minister, vindicated
the Mission from the aspersions and alleged grievances
of Mr. Jones, showed how that gentleman had dishonoured
his engagements, and proved that the services he had held
at the establishment of Mr. Jones at Waikouaiti were,
on his part, both voluntary and gratuitous. He pointed
out that the Wesleyan authorities in London had appointed

him to Otago and not to Waikouaiti ; that long ere Captain
Cargill's name had appeared before the public in the
office he now held in the Settlement, and long previous to
the arrival of any other minister in the district he had
been preaching at Port Chalmers and Dunedin and had
performed the rites and ceremonies of worship at Otago,
Taieri, the Molyneux and elsewhere. Moreover, when
Captain Cargill and the Scottish settlers arrived he was
found at his post, engaged in his Master's work and discharging his duties to both natives and Europeans without
reference to sect or party.

The worthy Captain erred through a curious incom-
pleteness of knowledge and an excess of denominational
zeal. He had not only made no attempt to understand
the facts but had omitted to note what the facts were.
The dignified statement of Mr. Creed convinced him
that it was just as hopeless to frame an effective rejoinder
as was an attempt to condense the morning mist into a
granite block.

Nevertheless Burns and Cargill and their associates
were men of enterprise, of endurance, of self-sacrifice
and of spiritual vision. With courage of heart and strength
of brain they laboured and reared a city where lordly pines
once raised their heads above a tangle of scrub. The very
memory of them stimulates high thought and noble passion
as we stoop to lay a garland at their feet.

Chapter XXII

BY WAY OF CONCLUSION

> He that ever following her commands,
> On with toil of heart and knees and hands,
> Thro' the long gorge to the far light has won
> His path upward, and prevail'd—
> Shall find the toppling crags of Duty scaled
> Are close upon the shining table-lands
> To which our God Himself is moon and sun.
> —ALFRED TENNYSON.

IT does not come within the scope of this volume to follow the fortunes of the Scottish Settlement or to chronicle the magnificent contribution made by the pilgrims of 1848 to the cause of colonization. The value of that contribution is beyond computation. Nor is it any part of the purpose of the book to deal with the consequences that flowed from the inrush of population through the opening of the goldfields of Otago. The stories of both the 'old identities' and the 'new iniquities' belong to the later period of settlement and have often been recited. Interest does attach, however, to the subsequent story of the mission to Southern Maoridom. This does not make inspiring reading and it may be briefly told.

Writing on September 4, 1851, Mr. Creed states that Christianity had accomplished wonders amongst the native people. It had subverted a complicated and powerful system of heathen worship. The sanguinary laws and practices of the cannibal had given place to mild and peaceful Christian usages. The musket and the tomahawk had been laid aside for the spade and the reaping hook. Obscene and horrible war songs and war dances had given place to the songs of Zion and assemblies for worshipping the true God. In spite of these successes Mr. Creed acknowledged that the Maori people were still in a state of transition from heathenism to semi-civilization. Whilst a few natives were more advanced their 'incipient Christianity' was being tested by 'the insidious attacks of evil disguised under a thousand forms.' The trying position in which the natives had been placed by the great influx of Europeans was aggravated by the abominable wickedness of some white men of unsteady habits who had settled in almost every native village. These men encouraged the Maoris to take strong drink and for their own evil ends sought to induce them to give up their religion. Many of the young men of Maoridom had proved all too apt imitators of the wicked practices of these degraded Europeans.

The work of Mr. Creed was sadly hampered by the size of his circuit, which made effective pastoral oversight extremely difficult. He was also hampered by the lack of an adequate staff of efficient Maori helpers, while the smallness of the number of natives now left in the villages made it practically impossible to maintain any proper system of instruction.

In this transition period, when the natives most needed shepherding, financial support from England was reduced to a degree that made it impracticable to sustain a trained and efficient staff of workers. The Wesleyan Methodist Missionary Society of England had spent about £180,000 in Maori evangelization in the North and South Islands down to the year 1855, and after this period the work was left to the churches in Australia and New Zealand, which were then constituted an independent Conference.

Meanwhile European settlers in the South were making insistent appeals for the ordinances of religion, and Mr. Creed recorded his judgement that if he had the labourers to enter the opening doors and to occupy the positions already gained 'Methodism would soon assume no mean standing in these districts.' Mr. Creed was transferred to the North Island in 1852, and save for the break of a year the Methodist Maori work was carried on until 1859, when the European missionary was withdrawn. Good service was rendered by the Revs. William Kirk and George Stannard and by various lay helpers and native teachers. From 1840 to 1859 the Wesleyan missionaries performed 896 baptisms and 201 marriages.

In 1859 a society was formed in Dunedin for ameliorating the physical, moral, religious, and social conditions of the Maori and half-caste population of the Province. This society was represented first by Mr. C. Baker, and afterwards, until 1867, by Mr. Reimenschneider, a devoted worker, who had married the daughter of the Rev. William Woon, a Wesleyan missionary. Mr. Reimenschneider had formerly, by arrangement with the Wesleyans, carried on a Lutheran mission at Pari-haka, where he commanded the respect of those turbulent chiefs, Te Whiti and Tohu.

About 1868 the Presbyterians took over the Maori work at Otago Heads, and were served for two years by the Rev. Alexander Blake. Subsequently Bishop Nevill sent the Rev. Edward Ngara, a native clergyman, to work in the same field. For some time after 1871 the Maoris themselves sustained the ordinances of religion amongst their own people. The Wesleyan native minister stationed at Rapaki paid occasional visits to the South until 1891, and oversight was later exercised from Colac Bay, and still more recently by occasional Maori ministers from the North Island and by the ministers of European churches contiguous to the native settlements. The Southern Maoris are few in number and the bright morning of Christian enterprise amongst them has been followed by a clouded evening sky.

Nevertheless the work amongst the Maoris has had its reflex influence upon the whole course of European life and colonization. The hours of the last decade of the first century of Christian enterprise in Southern Maoriland are steadily being marked off by the great time-piece in the heavens. Since Watkin began his work the years have passed with rushing swiftness. The past rises out of eternity and asserts itself. We cannot re-live it, nor can we erase its record and write it over again. We are under the tyranny of the tenses. The future looms before us and sounds a challenge like the bugle-call to a great campaign. From our yesterdays we cannot escape and to our to-morrows we dare not be indifferent. We stand in a great tradition. As we look over the rim of vanishing years and rehearse the great things of a proud though shadowed past, the swinging tides of emotion sway us towards the triumphs of to-morrow.

We are looking out upon a world in confusion, but it is a world exulting in new opportunities, seething with new ideas, holding to new hopes, rushing into new experiments. Life is taking on bigger meanings. Man is being crowned with new dignities. Another era is about to dawn. To-morrow is coming to us like a breath of morning air. Those who laid the foundations of community life in Southern Maoriland have fallen out of the ranks. The standard has dropped from their grasp. It is ours to keep it from trailing in the dust, ours to bear it to some nobler height. From our hands posterity will take its destiny. This hour is one that calls us to new ideals of citizenship, to new consecration, new expectancy, new ventures of faith. It bids us lay hold of our tasks, not that we may chase the glow of some elusive glory, but that we may make New Zealand—a country rich in resources and pregnant with possibilities—a land that shall, in days to be, become increasingly famed for the character of its institutions and for the moral beauty of its sons and daughters.

GLOSSARY OF MAORI WORDS

Atua	god, demon.
Haka	a dance.
Hapu	clan, section of a tribe.
Kaik, kaika	bivouac, quarters, place of abode.
Kapai rawa	very good.
Korero	discussion.
Kuri	a native dog.
Mana	prestige, influence.
Manes	psychic force, prestige.
Manuka	a tea tree shrub.
Maro	a kilt or apron.
Mere	a short stone weapon.
Muru	plunder, confiscation.
Pa	a stockade, fortified place.
Pakeha	foreigner.
Parai	beach
Parewata	payment, revenge.
Patu	a weapon for pounding.
Pipis	cockles.
Poi	a rhythmical dance.
Rangatira	a chief.
Raupo	bulrushes.
Tangi	a mourning.
Taniwhas	fabulous monsters.
Tapu	under restriction, sacred.
Taua	a war party.
Taula	an order of students for the priesthood.
Tiki	grotesque greenstone figure worn as an ornament.
Toas	warriors, braves.
Tohunga	priest, wizard.
Utu	ransom, reward.
Wahine	a woman, female.
Waiata tangi	a song of lamentation.
Whare	a house.
Whare karakia	a house of worship.

INDEX

AGRICULTURAL SETTLEMENT, 101, 102
Akaroa, Slaughter at, 38
   Catholics at, 141
   Creed at, 188, 204
   Selwyn at, 157
Aldred, Rev. John, 186, 202
American Vessels, 29, 67
   Whalers, 78
Anaru Tatairaki, 176, 178
Ancestor Worship, 78
Andersen, Mr. Johannes, 24
Anderson, John, 206
Anglican Native Teachers, 141
Anglican Sphere, 149
Apostolic Succession, 161, 163

BAKER, MR. C., 215
Baptisms, By Watkin, 131, 177
   First Public, 174, 175
   By Ironside, 187
   In Otago, 215
Bells, 124, 125
Best, Mr. Elsdon, 17, 23
Bible Society, 126, 161
Blake, Rev. Alexander, 215
Blood Lust, 93
' Bloody Jack ' (See also Tuhawaiki), 165
Bluff, Watkin at, 137
Book, First in South Island Dialect, 114
   Magical, 82, 83
British Sovereignty, Prior to, 50, 64
     In prospect, 65
     Consent sought for, 66
     Proclaimed, 62
     Approved, 68
     In operation, 90
Browning quoted, 27, 36, 47, 56
Buick, Mr. Lindsay, 17, 69
Buller, Sir Walter, 197
Bumby, Rev. J. H., Visits Sydney, 48
     Inaugurates mission, 149
     Arrival of, 203

Bunbury, Major, 109
Bunting, Rev. Jabez, 51
Burials, Of Native woman, 73
          Of Mr. and Mrs. Thomas, 73
          First Christian, 174
Burns, Rev. Thomas, 207, 210, 212

CANNIBALISM, 39, 42, 46, 87, 148
Canterbury Settlement, 64
Cargill, Captain W., 211, 212
Carruth, Professor, quoted, 76
Chapel at Waikouaiti, 146, 175, 176
Chimney (First in South Island), 103
Christchurch, Site of, passed, 205
Christmas Feast, 177
Clarke, George, In Hobart, 15
                Interpreter, 15
                Otago Deed of Purchase, 15
Cloudy Bay, War expedition, 32, 43
          Mission at, 145, 147, 186
Communication, Difficulty of, 123
Communion, First Observance, 125
          Selwyn and, 162
          Maoris at, 177
Cook, Captain James, 87
Cowan, Mr. James, 17, 25
Creed, Charles, at Waikouaiti, 17, 23
                Korako converted through, 88
                Lost on Banks Peninsula, 188
                Arrival at Waikouaiti, 189
                Area worked by, 202
                Travels of, 202, 204, 205
                Report and Record of, 213
                Grave of, 63
Creed, Mrs., Instructs Natives, 23
            Assists Wohlers, 192
Cripples, Belief concerning, 82
Crocome, Joseph, 180
Cross, Rev. William, 58

DANTE QUOTED, 81
Death, of Tautaki, 72, 82
       Hopeless grief at, 90
       Maori belief, 91
       of Kahu, 93
       of Tokonui, 174
Depopulation, 99
Diseases, Influenza, 44
          Play havoc, 45
          Venereal, &c., 100
          Measles, 100, 166

Drink, Evils of, 29, 70, 73, 74, 75, 168
Drinkwater, John, quoted, 195
Duncan, Rev. J., 198
Dunedin, Description of in 1845, 205
    Creed's first visit to, 205
    First baptism at, 206
    First births at, 206
    First religious services at, 206
D'Urville, Dumont, 34, 66
D'Urville Island, Slaughter at, 36
Dutch Vessels, 29
Dying, Treatment of, 73

EDUCATION, Pioneer of, 116
Egglestone, Rev. John, 213
Entwisle, Rev. Joseph, 58, 59, 181
Epiha Putini, 155

FAIRCLOUGH, REV. P. W., 160
Famine, threatened, 104
Fenton, Rev. J. A., 162, 209
Fenwick, Sir George, 17
Ferens, Mr. Thomas, 204, 207
Fiji, Plea for, 59, 184
FitzRoy, Governor, 15, 154
Flaxbourne River, Battle at, 43
Foreign Invasion, 99
France, King of, 139
Francis, Rev. Robert, quoted, 128
Franklin, Sir John, 203
French Emigrants, 139
French Vessels, 67
Future possibilities, 216

GARDINER, MR. FLORENCE, 16
Gipps, Governor, Chiefs interview, 50
    Controls New Zealand, 65
    Gift to Tuhawaiki, 167
Gods, many, 79
  Capricious, 80
Goldfields, 213
Grasmere Lake, Fight at, 42
Grey, Governor Sir George, 62, 196, 199

HADFIELD, REV. OCTAVIUS, Sends Natives South, 142
    Arrival in New Zealand, 151
    Enters Wesleyan sphere, 48, 151
Hardships, 104
Harmonium, 125
Headlam, Dr., quoted, 163
Heads, tattooed, 94, 148

Herd, Captain James, 64
Hoani Weteri Korako, 180
Hobart Town shipping merchants, 28, 29
Hobbs, Rev. John, At Cook's Straits, 149
                        At Bay of Islands, 154
                        At Selwyn's farewell, 162
Hobson, Governor, 16, 65, 68
Hocken, Dr. T. M., 13, 209
Hohepa Maru, 204
Horomona Pohio, 179

INFANTICIDE, 92, 93
Inge, Dean, quoted, 163
Io, Supreme God, 76
Ironside, Rev. Samuel, In Hobart, 15, 203
                        At Hokianga, 48
                        Friend of Watkin, 61, 109, 142, 158, 159
                        At Cloudy Bay, 70, 122, 141, 185, 202
                        Preaching squads of, 143, 202
                        Converts of, 144, 147, 175
                        Sends Testaments, 161
                        Warns Wakefield, 185
                        Fears realized, 186
                        At Tua Marina, 186
                        Buries victims of Massacre, 186
                        Mission smashed, 187, 202
                        In Wellington, 187, 202
                        Commends Wohlers, 187

JACKEY WHITE (see Karetai),
Jacob's River, visited, 116, 137
Jones, Mr. John, Whaling Stations, 30
                        Acquires Land, 30
                        Seeks a missionary, 49
                        Answered by Creed, 211
Jones, Mr. Thomas, 102

KAHU, DEATH OF, 93
Kaiapoi, Attack upon, 37, 38
                Sacking of, 39, 41
Kapiti, Watkin designated for, 48, 150
        Te Rauparaha at, 36, 37, 39, 42, 150
Karetai, At Lake Grasmere, 42
                At Little River, 46
                In Sydney, 65
                Marriages of, 171
Karitane Peninsula, 21, 24
                Origin of name, 22, 23
Kehu, 166
Kelly, Captain James, Offends Maoris, 31
                        Revenge on, 32

Kettle, Mr. C. H., 206
King George I. of Tonga, 105
King, Sir Truby, 23
King William IV., Petition to, 64
Kirk, Rev. William, 215
Korako, Outraged, 34
        Discussion with, 78, 100
        Prowess of, 87
        Baptized, 88
        Bereaved, 88
Kurakura, Drowning of, 89
        Discussion with, 100

LAMB, CHARLES, quoted, 81
Lambeth Conference, 163
Land Conveyance, first, 43
Land transactions, Forbidden to Wesleyan missionaries, 197
        Purchases, 65, 69, 101, 196
        Otago Block, 15, 166, 199, 200
        Sales, 43, 65, 197
Language (Maori), Vocabulary, 108
        Divergent dialect, 108, 110
        Unwritten dialect, 110
        Instability of, 110
        Inadequacy of, 112
        Preaching in, 113
Lawry, Rev. Walter, 58
Lay Association, 198
Leigh, Rev. Samuel, 148
Lovett, Captain W., Crews attacked, 31, 32

MACKAY, MISS JESSIE, quoted, 202
Mahaka, Baptism of, 175
Mantell, Mr. Walter, 197
Maoris, Religious beliefs of, 76, 78, 84, 91
        Mythology of, 72
        Folk lore of, 77, 78
        Nature worshippers, 79
        Family life, 98, 120
        Dwellings of, 120
        Clothing of, 119
        Pursuits of, 121
        Wars, 69
        In Stone Age, 98
        Capricious, 93
        Ungrateful, 121
        Indolent, 121
        Character of, 118
        Priests, 77
        Resent foreign intrusion, 86
        Women and Girls, 70, 99, 121, 177
        Elevation of, 127, 138, 175, 181, 193, 201, 213

Marriages, Anglo–Maori, 124, 131, 136
       Maori, 116, 124, 131
       Plural, 88, 171
       In Otago, 215
Marsden, Rev. Samuel, 148, 198
Maru, 180
Massacre, at Wairau, 15, 147, 185
       at Tuturau, 45, 165, 166, 179
       at Akaroa, 38
Matene Ti Whiwhi, 143, 144
Matiaha Tiromorehu, 176, 177
Mau Mau, Rev. Apollos, 60
McNab, Dr. Robert, 13, 17, 102, 109
Measles, 44, 100, 166
Medicine dispensed, 134
Merekihireka Hape, 171
Merrington, Dr., quoted, 211
Mieville, Mr. F. L., quoted, 209
Milne, Captain, 60
Milton, quoted, 86
Mission House, Site of, 96
       Occupants of, 102, 103
Moeraki, Boulders, 21
       Battle at, 24
       Work at, 132, 133
       Tradition, 133
       Catholics at, 140
       Wohlers at, 145
       Shortland visits, 145
       Selwyn at, 157
Molyneux, Port, 100
       River, 167
       Creed at, 212
Monro, Dr. David, 169
Monson, Mr. Henry, 207
Moral Standards, 99
Moran, Cardinal, 141
Moseley, Mr. W. A., 210
Mount Watkin, name given, 22, 97
Muru, law of, 94, 170
Music, 125
Myers, F. W. H., quoted, 118

NATIVE ASSESSORS, 173
Native chiefs, 173
Native teachers, 127, 133, 181
Nature, capricious, 79
       personified, 79
Neale, Rev. E. J., 209
Nelson Settlement, 64
Nene, Tamata Waaka, 68

New iniquities, 213
New Testaments, 126, 160, 203
New Zealand, Mythical period, 19
            Legendary period, 19
            Traditional period, 20
            Historical period, 21
            Settlement of, 64
            British Sovereignty, 67, 68
New Zealand Company, 198
Nevill, Bishop, 215
Ngai-Tahu tribe, displaced Ngatimamoe, 20
            Came from North, 21
            Hapus at Karitane, 24
            Attacked, 36, 37, 41
            Tribal deity, 77
Ngara, Rev. Edward, 215
Ngatimamoe tribe, Invasion by, 20
            At Moeraki, 24
Nias, Captain, 67
Nicholson, Rev. T. D. 207
Noa Paka, 100

Ogres, 19, 80
Old identities, 213
Onawe, Slaughter at, 41
Otago Block, Purchase of, 15, 166, 199, 200
Otago Goldfields, 213
Outrages against Maoris, by Captain Kelly, 31
            by Brown, 33
            Kidnapping, 34
            Against Korako, 34
            by John McGregor, 69
            on Native Boy, 74

Palmer, Edward, 189
Palmer, James, 175
Paremata, Law of, 121
Park, Mr. Robert, 206
Plumptre, Dean, E. H., quoted, 148
Pompallier, Bishop, at Otago, 83, 109, 139–141, 211
            at Moeraki, 157
Pope, quoted, 81
Pope, Gregory XVI., 139
Portuguese vessels, 29
Pratt, Mr. A. W. Courtney, 18
Presbyterian Advent, 198

Queen's College, Melbourne, 16

Rawiri, Kingi Puaha, Wesleyan Teacher, 147
            Plea for peace, 185, 186

Rawiri, Te Maire, Native Teacher, 23
                    with Watkin, 131
                    Biography of, 179
                    Accompanies Creed, 204
Rawiri Waiteri Mamaru, 171, 176
Reimenschneider, Mr., 215
Religious Beliefs of Maoris (See Maoris)
Religious Unity, 149
Richardson, Mr., at Wairau, 186
Roberts Mr. W. H. S., 22
Roman Catholics (See also Pompallier)
                    In Dunedin, 141
                    Mission of, 198
Ross, Mr. Donald, 207, 210
Ruapuke, Visited, 136
            Described, 137
            Strife at, 146, 190
            Wohlers at, 190

SABBATH OBSERVANCE, by Maoris, 123, 172, 178
Sacrifices, human, 78, 86, 88, 89
Schools established Mission, 113, 114, 116
                    Free Church, 117
Scottish Settlement, Search for site, 188
                    Project for, 198
                    Lay Association, 198
                    Scheme delayed, 198
                    Site chosen, 199
                    A Class colony, 210
Sealing Industry, 27, 28
Sectarian differences, 142, 163
Selwyn, Bishop, At Waikouaiti, 109
                    Confirms Tamihana, 147
                    Policy of, 152
                    Travels and effects, 157–161, 211
Sermon, First, 120
            First extempore, 113
Shakespeare, quoted, 174
Sham fight, Maori, 94
Ships mentioned— Amity, 31
                    Astrolabe, 66
                    Deborah, 62, 187, 199
                    Derwent Hunter, 18
                    Elizabeth, 37
                    Herald, 68, 109
                    James, 203
                    John Wickliffe, 201, 206
                    Juliana, 122
                    Lancaster, 122
                    Lloyds, 58
                    Magnet, 49, 66

Ships mentioned — Martha, 149
                   Mary and Elizabeth, 32
                   Minerva, 60
                   New England, 63
                   Orientel, 34
                   Pacific, 18
                   Pearl, 170
                   Pelorus, 151
                   Philip Laing, 201
                   Regia, 50
                   Rosanna, 64
                   Sancta Maria, 139
                   Scotia, 136
                   St. Pauli, 185
                   Sophia, 31
                   Sydney Packet, 44, 100
                   Triton, 122, 203
                   Zelee, 66
Shortland, Dr., 145
Skevington, Rev. J. S., 156
Smith, Captain W. M., 198
Spencer, James, 136
Stannard, Rev. George, 215
Stewart Island, visited, 137
Stewart, John, 38
Stone Age, 98
Strode, Mr. A. R. C., 210
Strode, Sir E. C., 210
Strong Drink, 70, 74, 75, 168
Superstition challenged, 83
Swing, native, 98
Sydney, Shipping Merchants, 28
        Seat of Government, 68
        Maori Hostages in, 32
        Chiefs wish to visit, 46
        Watkin at, 60
        Chiefs at, 65
Sym, Rev. John, 209

TAAWAO, Native teacher, 141
Taiaroa, Te Matenga, Relieves Kaiapoi, 40
                      Leaves Kaiapoi, 40
                      Attacks Te Rauparaha, 43
                      Attacks Whaling Station, 43
                      At Tuturau, 45
                      Signs Treaty, 67
                      Ancestry, 169
                      Baptized, 171
                      at Akaroa, 187
Taieri, Watkin at, 136
        Creed at, 212

Taipo, 99

Takatahara, Slays Te Pehi, 37
　　　　　Interviews Watkin 38
　　　　　Defeated at Onawe, 42
　　　　　Released by Te Hiko, 42

Tamaiharanui Defends Kaiapoi, 37
　　　　　Beguiled by Stewart, 38
　　　　　Daughter Strangled, 39
　　　　　Son killed, 39
　　　　　Eaten, 39
　　　　　Attempt to avenge, 44

Tamati Waaka Nene, 68

Tamihana, Visits Otago, 143, 144, 146
　　　　　Confirmation of, 147
　　　　　At Bay of Islands, 151
　　　　　At Temuka, 157
　　　　　At Ruapuke, 159
　　　　　In controversy, 160

Taoka, Struggle with Te Wera, 24, 26
Tapu, Law of, 73
Tasman, Abel Janzoon, 21
Tattooed heads sold, 94, 148
Taufa-ahau, King of Tonga, 59. 105
Tautaki, Death of, 72
Te Awaitai, 154
Te Hiko, 38, 42
Te Kooti, 14
Tennyson quoted, 96, 157, 213
Temuka, 143, 157, 172, 205
Te Pehi Kupe, Joins Te Rauparaha, 36
　　　　　Killed at Kaiapoi, 37
　　　　　Widow's Revenge, 39
　　　　　Son's action, 42

Te Puohu's raid, 44, 45, 179

Te Rauparaha, Repulsed at Kaiapoi, 37
　　　　　Attacks Akaroa, 38
　　　　　His ambition, 36
　　　　　Victory at Kaikoura, 37
　　　　　Victory at D'Urville Island, 36
　　　　　Destroys Kaiapoi, 40
　　　　　Attacks Onawe, 41
　　　　　Attacked at Grasmere, 42
　　　　　Attacked at Queen Charlotte Sound 43
　　　　　Seeks peace, 46
　　　　　Son of, 143, 144
　　　　　Record of, 150
　　　　　Tuhawaiki and, 168
　　　　　At Wairau Massacre, 185

Teuteraki Pauwa, Outraged and Suicide of, 33

Te Wera, At Waikouaiti, 25
   Attacked, 26
   Death of, 26
Te Whakataupuka, Attacks Weller's Station, 32
      Sells land, 43
      Death of, 166
Te Whiti, 215
Thomas, Mr. W. G., 73, 90
Thomas, Rev. John, 58
Thompson, Surveyor at Wairau, 186
Tiare Weteri Te Kahu, 131, 180
Tione Topi Patuki, Shoots Te Puohu, 45
     In training, 146
     Wesleyan teacher, 171
Tohiti Haereroa, 172
Tohu, 215
Tohungas, Powers of, 97
Tommy Roundhead, (See also Tohiti Haereroa), 172
Tonga, 58–60, 175
Tracy, Mona, quoted, 165
Travels, of Watkin, 128–138
   of Creed, 204, 205
Trench, Archbishop, quoted, 108
Tucker, Rev. H. W., 160
Tuckett, Frederick, 169, 187, 199
Tuhawaiki, At Lake Grasmere, 42
   At Flaxbourne River, 43
   Succeeds his Uncle, 44
   Northward Expedition, 45
   At Little River, 46
   In Sydney, 65
   Signs Treaty, 67
   Biographical Sketch, 165
   Bodyguard, 187
   At Akaroa, 169
   Death of 169
   Son's death, 169
Turner, Rev. Nathaniel, 58
Turton, Rev. H. H., 155
Tuturau Massacre, 44, 165, 167, 179

Union Jack Hoisted, 68

Vocabulary, 108, 112, 172

Waikouaiti, Watkin at, 16
   Bay, 21
   Whaling Station, 96
   Borough, 96
   Moral Standards, 70
Wairau Massacre, 15, 147, 185, 186, 202

Waitaha, Tribe in South, 20
Waitangi, Treaty of, 67, 68
Wakefield, Captain, 185
Wakefield, Colonel, 15, 185, 199, 200
Wakefield, E. G., View of Colonization, 195
Wallis, Rev. James, 162
Warren, Rev. John, 203
Waterhouse, Rev. John, 203
Watkin, Edwin Iredale, 16, 102, 105
Watkin, Jabez Bunting, 16, 102, 105
Watkin, Rev. James, At Waikouaiti, 16, 22, 33, 54, 55, 67
     Biography, 57–63
     Oxford training refused, 57
     Appointment to Tonga, 58
     Voyage from England, 58
     At Bay of Islands, 58, 60
     In Sydney, 61
     Designated for Kapiti, 150
     Appointment to New Zealand, 48
     Voyage to New Zealand, 50
     Children of, 102, 106
     First service, 119
     Learning the language, 108–116
     Educational Pioneer, 117
     Difficulties of, 75
     Illness, 106, 123
     Isolation, 122
     Travels, 128–138
     Journal, 57, 68, 72, 140, 142
     Successes, 62, 106, 138, 159, 180, 201
     Reviled, 71, 74
     Removal to Wellington, 201
     Shipwrecked, 63
     Death of, 63
Watkin, James, Junior, 102, 115
Watkin, John Wesley, 106
Watkin, Joseph Hebblewhite, 106
Watkin, Mrs., 51, 58, 74, 102, 106
Watkin, Rev. W. J., 63, 102, 105, 115
Watson, Rev. Richard, 57
Wentworth, Mr. W. C., 66
Wesley, John, 163, 195
Wesleyan Missions, Official Tribute to, 173, 197
     Wakefield's Tribute, 195
     Roosevelt's tribute, 195
     Dr. Lang's tribute 197
     Mr. Mantell's tribute, 197
     House of Commons Report, 197
Wesleyan Prayer Book, 208
Wesleyan sphere, 149
Whalers, 27, 32, 48, 69, 85

Whaling, 27, 28, 30, 32, 44, 64, 96
Whangaroa, Mission Station destroyed, 94
Whateley, Archbishop, 163
White, Rev. William, 149
Whyte, Rev. Alexander, 200
Widow, Strangling of, 91
        Lament by, 91
Wilberforce, 57
Wilcox, Dora, quoted, 19
Williams, Mr. E. M., 109
Williams, Peter, Land purchased by, 43
Williams, Rev. Henry, 151
Williams, Rev. W. J., 153
Wiremu Nera, 154
Wiremu Patene, 204
Wohlers, Rev. J. F. H., Influenced, 60
                Comes South, 145
                Biography of, 183–194
                Alluded to, 222
Woon, Rev. William, 215
Wordsworth, quoted, 81
' Wrymouth ' (Kurakura), 77